BABAK ANVARI

Babak Anvari is a BAFTA-winning writer/director based in London. His debut feature, *Under the Shadow*, which he wrote and directed, was the UK's submission for the Academy Award for Best Foreign Language Film and won the BAFTA for Outstanding Debut in 2017. The film was also nominated for Outstanding British Film that same year, alongside numerous international festival awards including the New Visions Award at Sitges.

His subsequent work includes *Wounds*, adapted from Nathan Ballingrud's novella *The Visible Filth*, which premiered at Sundance and had its European premiere in Directors' Fortnight at Cannes; Hulu's *Monsterland*, on which he served as executive producer and directed the finale; and the Netflix thriller *I Came By*, which he co-wrote and directed. Most recently, he directed *Hallow Road*, starring Rosamund Pike and Matthew Rhys, which premiered at SXSW in 2025 to critical acclaim.

CARMEN NASR

Carmen Nasr is British Lebanese writer. Her previous work includes the breakout play *Dubailand* (Finborough Theatre, 2018) and *The Climbers*, directed by Guy Jones (Theatre by the Lake, 2022). She has also created ensemble-led work including *The Maladies* (Almeida Young Company/The Yard, 2022); *Let Kilburn Shake* (Kiln Theatre's Young Company, 2018) and *I Am Lysistrata* (Makani/Park Theatre, 2024).

She was awarded the prestigious Channel 4 Playwrights' Scheme in 2017, and her early play *The House of My Father* was longlisted for the Bruntwood Prize. Her work has been supported by leading development programmes including the Royal Court Playwriting Group and the Orange Tree Writers Collective. For screen, she is developing her first original TV project with support from Sky Productions.

Babak Anvari

UNDER THE SHADOW

Adapted for the stage by

Carmen Nasr

NICK HERN BOOKS

London
www.nickhernbooks.co.uk

A Nick Hern Book

Under the Shadow first published in Great Britain as a paperback original in 2026 by Nick Hern Books Limited, The Glasshouse, 49a Goldhawk Road, London W12 8QP

Under the Shadow (film) copyright © 2016 Babak Anvari, Two and Two Pictures
Under the Shadow (play) copyright © 2026 Carmen Nasr

Carmen Nasr has asserted her right to be identified as the author of this adaptation

Cover image of Leila Farzad, photographed by Nadav Kander.

Designed and typeset by Nick Hern Books, London
Printed in Great Britain by Mimeo Ltd, Huntingdon, Cambridgeshire PE29 6XX

A CIP catalogue record for this book is available from the British Library

ISBN 978 1 83904 521 9

www.nickhernbooks.co.uk/environmental-policy

Nick Hern Books' authorised representative in the EU is
Easy Access System Europe – Mustamäe tee 50, 10621 Tallinn, Estonia
email gpsr.requests@easproject.com

Under the Shadow was first performed at the Almeida Theatre, London, on 9 June 2026 (previews from 2 June). The cast was as follows:

PARGOL/SECRETARY	Nadia Albina
MR BIJARI/DIRECTOR	Bijan Daneshmand
MRS FAKUR	Souad Faress
SHIDEH	Leila Farzad
MRS EBRAHIMI	Mona Goodwin
IRAJ	Nicholas Karimi
MR EBRAHIMI/DOCTOR	Rachid Sabitri
DORSA	Esma Akar
	Atlanta Chaniac Golding
	Erin Jemmotte
MEHDI	Jago Agrawal
	Rohan Berry
	Adi Gimziunas

Creator of Original Film	Babak Anvari
Adaptor	Carmen Nasr
Director	Nadia Latif
Set Designer	Ben Stones
Costume Designer	Khadija Raza
Lighting Designer	James Farncombe
Sound Designer	Donato Wharton
Casting Director	Anna Cooper CDG
Children's Casting Director	Amy Beadle CDG
Illusion Consultant	Scott Penrose
Fight Director	Kev McCurdy
Movement Director	Malik Nashad Sharpe
Costume Supervisor	Olivia Ward
Props Supervisor	Mary Halliday
Assistant Director	Layla Madanat
Dramatherapist	Dr Sara Alsaraf

Acknowledgements

Thank you to Stephanie Bain, Nadia Latif, Rupert Goold, Dominic Cooke, Lucan Toh, Bryan Sonderman, Dan Rebellato, Jago Irwin, Sarah Williams, Stevie Jackson, Farzaneh Sabetkasei, Mostafa Anvari, Christine and Mo. For their contributions to the development of the play.

C.N.

Characters

SHIDEH, *thirty-seven, stay-at-home mother*
IRAJ, *thirty-eight, doctor*
DORSA, *seven, Shideh and Iraj's daughter*
MRS FAKUR, *sixty-two, retired professor, widow*
MRS EBRAHIMI, *thirty, housewife, heavily pregnant*
MR EBRAHIMI, *thirty-five, landlord and shopkeeper*
MEHDI, *twelve, orphan, Mr Ebrahimi's nephew*
PARGOL, *forty, unmarried, full-time carer to her father*
MR BIJARI, *seventy-nine, frail and elderly, Pargol's father*

and

SECRETARY
DOCTOR
DIRECTOR
PARAMEDICS/STUDENTS

and

DJINN

Notes on the Text

A dash (–) at the end of a line indicates an unfinished thought.

A forward slash (/) marks the point in a line where the following line interrupts or overlaps.

An ellipsis (…) at the end of the line indicates a trailing-off of the sentence.

An ellipsis (…) between lines indicates a pause.

This text went to press before the end of rehearsals and so may differ slightly from the play as performed.

ACT ONE

Prologue

Iran. 1988. Early March. An apartment in Tehran.

It's the middle of the night. Silence. Darkness. A boy, MEHDI, stands alone in the living room.

A low buzzing is heard, which gets progressively louder. It might be the sound of bombing in the distance, or a plane, or a storm brewing. MEHDI stares at the ceiling, transfixed. He very slowly lifts his arm, until he is reaching above his head towards the ceiling, as if pulled by an invisible force.

Suddenly the television comes on, blaring static and white noise. MEHDI stares at the TV. The static tunes into a state-sponsored news report on the current Iran–Iraq war. Images of the Iran–Iraq war and state propaganda illuminate MEHDI.

A dark shadow suddenly sweeps across the room, enveloping it in momentary darkness. When the shadow passes, MEHDI has vanished.

Scene One

Late morning. The apartment is now bathed in daylight.

Open-plan living and dining room. It's comfortable, middle-class, modern, but with the odd hint of formality. There are sofas, a television, telephone, coffee table, lamps, books, family photos, house plants. A warm palette of oranges and yellows. There are heavy curtains framing the windows, a dark wooden dining table covered with a tablecloth, and warm patterned rugs. We can see the front door and a hallway. A mirror hangs on the wall near the door, there is also a place for keys and coats.

At the back of the living area there are windows looking out onto the street below. Part of the kitchen can be seen through a doorway. There is a bin visible at the entrance to the kitchen. There is a door or a corridor leading off into the bedrooms. The apartment is meticulously tidy, except for a few toys, out of place, scattered on a corner of the carpet.

The television is on. Images and sounds of the Iran–Iraq war on a local news channel play out into the empty living room.

SHIDEH walks in from the corridor. She wears a T-shirt and leggings, she stops at the living room mirror, ties her hair up, inspects her face. She notices the TV is on. She doesn't remember turning it on. She shrugs, walks over and turns it off.

She prepares the room for her workout, a familiar ritual. The faint sound of shelling can almost be made out in the distance. She draws the curtains on all the windows. She shuts everything out.

She makes space in front of the TV area, moves a coffee table or an arm chair out of the way. She notices something is out of place and fixes it, straightens a painting, centres a vase. As she walks back to the TV, she accidentally steps on one of the toys and cries out in pain. She nurses her foot, picks up the toy and throws it across the room, then tidies the rest of the toys away into a wooden toybox.

She uncovers the video player from where it is hidden away under the TV. She pulls out a hidden box of videos and selects one, pops into the machine. It starts to play. It's Jane Fonda's workout tape from 1982. It beams out of the TV, filling the curtained living room with artificial light. SHIDEH starts working out to the tape. She moves intensely, the moves come to her effortlessly, as if she's done them a thousand times before.

She moves. She works up a sweat.

She moves. Harder.

She's in full flow.

And for a moment she begins to feel free...

The phone rings.

She ignores it. She lets it ring out.

The phone rings again. SHIDEH *gives in, pauses the tape and marches over to the phone. She picks it up, flustered, out of breath.*

SHIDEH. Hello?

…

No no I'm fine, just doing some exercises.

…

Yeah, Jane Fonda, how did yo–

…

He's still at the hospital, should be back soon though. Shall I get him to call you ba–

…

No, she's playing at the neighbour's downstairs.

…

Why don't I tell Iraj to call you back when him and Dorsa get ho–

…

Oh don't worry about us, it's actually really quiet in Tehran –

…

That's all rumours, I don't think –

…

Thank you, that's very kind, but we're fine here, we're –

…

Hold on. I can hear someone knocking on the door, I better –

…

Of course. No don't worry. I'll tell Iraj to call you. Goodbye. Bye.

She hangs up the phone. Rolls her eyes. She goes back to the video player. She presses play.

She moves.

She moves harder.

She's in full flow…

The doorbell rings.

SHIDEH *gives up on her workout. She stops the video, turns off the TV, covers the video player and puts the box of tapes back in their hiding place. The doorbell again.*

She walks over to the door and grabs her headscarf from the coat rack. She looks through the peephole, discards the scarf. She opens the door. It's MRS FAKUR, *neighbour, friend, confidante. She's dressed to go out; coat, bag and a headscarf loose around her neck. She holds an empty Pyrex dish in her hands.*

Oh it's you.

MRS FAKUR *comes inside.*

MRS FAKUR. No need to sound so disappointed.

SHIDEH. I thought it was Mr Ebrahimi for the rent.

MRS FAKUR. Why are you hyperventilating?

SHIDEH. I was exercising.

SHIDEH *walks over to the windows and draws the curtains open. As she chats to* MRS FAKUR, *she puts the room back as it was.*

MRS FAKUR. Good for you. I wish I had exercised when I was your age. Too late now.

SHIDEH. It's never too late.

MRS FAKUR. That's something only young people ever say.

SHIDEH. I'm not young.

MRS FAKUR. Also something only young people ever say.

Where's Dorsa?

SHIDEH. At the Ebrahimis' playing with the new kid, the nephew, what's his name? A bit weird. Stares a lot.

MRS FAKUR. Mehdi.

SHIDEH. That's right.

Tea?

MRS FAKUR. No no no. I'm on my way to the shops. Just dropping this off.

MRS FAKUR *holds out the Pyrex dish.* SHIDEH *takes it, inspects it and hands it back.*

SHIDEH. That's not mine.

MRS FAKUR. Yes it is. I borrowed it last week.

SHIDEH. Not from me.

MRS FAKUR. Oh it must be Pargol's then. Silly me. You see what happens when you're actually old? It's an absolute nightmare. Brain like a sieve.

SHIDEH. How is Pargol? I've been meaning to go up.

MRS FAKUR. She's stopped speaking to Mrs Ebrahimi.

SHIDEH. Again?

MRS FAKUR. Apparently, Pargol confided in her about her poor father's incontinence, begged her not to breathe a word to anyone, but then Mrs Ebrahimi goes and leaves a big packet of adult nappies right on their doorstep, in plain sight, for everyone to see, and of course Pargol's convinced she did it on purpose.

SHIDEH. I'm sure she was only trying to be helpful.

MRS FAKUR. I told her, that woman's got the tact of an ox, but she means well. I know, me defending Mrs Ebrahimi? But that Pargol, she can be so headstrong.

SHIDEH. She's just stressed, she's overwhelmed, seeing your own parent like that, day in and day out, it's not easy.

MRS FAKUR. You know my husband used to say that the Kurds are terribly stubborn. I'd tell him off of course. Or was it the Armenians who were stubborn, and the Kurds who were – anyway, look at us gossiping like housewives, how shameful, I better go and drop this off to its rightful owner.

SHIDEH *follows* MRS FAKUR *to the door, but* MRS FAKUR *hesitates.*

Oh, I forgot to say…

SHIDEH. To say what?

MRS FAKUR. Well it's just that…

MRS FAKUR *can't bring herself to say it.*

SHIDEH. Mrs Fakur, what is it?

MRS FAKUR. I heard back from my cousin, Omid.

SHIDEH. And?

MRS FAKUR *shakes her head sadly.*

What does that mean?

MRS FAKUR. You're on a list.

SHIDEH. For how long?

MRS FAKUR. I don't know. Nobody really knows.

SHIDEH. Does he think my name can ever come off that list?

MRS FAKUR. He didn't say.

SHIDEH. What were his actual words?

MRS FAKUR. I don't remember exactly, Shideh. I can barely remember who I borrowed this dish from.

SHIDEH. Please, Mrs Fakur.

MRS FAKUR. He said something like, they will probably never let her back into medical school and, well, tell her to get on with her life.

SHIDEH *sits on the sofa. She holds back her tears.* MRS FAKUR *thinks of something useful to say.*

You have your whole life ahead of you.

SHIDEH. Exactly. Day after day of this. Always this. Again and again and again –

MRS FAKUR. Oh you mustn't despair Shideh. Despair never did anyone any good. And I should know, twenty years of teaching and –

SHIDEH. I can't do it, waking up every day, nowhere to go, nothing to do.

MRS FAKUR. Well whatever you do, don't get used to it. That was my mistake. Keep fighting.

SHIDEH. But I've tried everything.

MRS FAKUR. You have your home, your health. You have Iraj, and beautiful Dorsa.

This sends SHIDEH *deeper into despair, she holds her head in her hands.* MRS FAKUR *strokes her hair.*

Oh Shideh.

DORSA *enters through the front door.* SHIDEH *composes herself.*

SHIDEH. Hello, my love.

MRS FAKUR. Dorsa!

They each get a hug from DORSA.

DORSA. Look, Mehdi gave me a ball of fur from a baby cat.

MRS FAKUR. You mean a kitten.

DORSA *shoves a little dirty ball of fur into* SHIDEH*'s face. It stinks.*

SHIDEH. Oh Dorsa, it stinks.

DORSA. No it doesn't.

SHIDEH. Throw it in the bin.

DORSA. No! It's mine.

SHIDEH. It's filthy. God knows what's in there, it's probably rat fur.

DORSA. Rats aren't fluffy.

MRS FAKUR. Listen to your mum, Dorsa. You're a good girl.

DORSA. But it's magic fur. Look!

DORSA tries to show MRS FAKUR, *who moves away in disgust.*

SHIDEH. It belongs in the bin.

DORSA. It's going to protect me.

SHIDEH. From what?

DORSA. Bad stuff.

SHIDEH. Give it to me.

DORSA holds the furball away from SHIDEH *protectively, then walks off and finds a spot to play.*

MRS FAKUR. I'd better go. Will you be okay?

SHIDEH. I'm fine.

MRS FAKUR. Remember. Don't get used to it.

MRS FAKUR leaves. SHIDEH *gathers herself. Deep breath.*

SHIDEH. Go and wash your hands, Dorsa.

DORSA. I'm not throwing it away.

SHIDEH. Fine.

DORSA goes back to playing with her toys. SHIDEH *goes to the kitchen. She gets a roll of bin bags. She walks back to the living room and starts to angrily remove books from the bookshelf and throw them in the bin bag.* DORSA *notices the books.*

DORSA. Why are you throwing away your books?

SHIDEH. We need more space.

DORSA. What for?

SHIDEH. I don't know. Other things.

SHIDEH carries on with determination. She picks up a big book and hesitates. A special book, the Guyton and Hall Textbook of Medical Physiology, *in English. She goes to put it in the bin bag.*

DORSA. No! That's the special book from Granny.

DORSA *grabs it from* SHIDEH*'s hands.*

She said I could have it when I'm older.

DORSA *sits down with the book and opens it up to the first page. She starts to read as best she can.*

To my daughter. Congratu–, congratu-la-tions – on medi– medical –

SHIDEH. That's enough.

SHIDEH *takes the book from* DORSA.

DORSA. Did Grandma have a job?

SHIDEH. She was a housewife.

DORSA. What's a housewife?

SHIDEH. Go and wash your hands.

DORSA. Are you a housewife?

SHIDEH. No.

DORSA *holds up the book again.*

DORSA. Promise to keep this one?

SHIDEH. I promise.

DORSA *hands* SHIDEH *the book.* SHIDEH *tries to smile.*

DORSA. Why are you sad?

SHIDEH. I'm not sad, I'm just tired of being asked a million and one questions every ten minutes.

DORSA. Do you want me to tell you a joke?

SHIDEH. Go on then.

DORSA. Why did the shirt drink tea?

SHIDEH. I don't know. Why?

DORSA. It's a T-shirt! It loves tea.

SHIDEH softens. She smiles, gives DORSA a cuddle or a kiss.

Do you want to hear another one?

SHIDEH. Why don't you save it for Baba? Go and tidy away the toys in your room before lunch. Good girl.

SHIDEH gives her a kiss. DORSA skips off to her bedroom. SHIDEH looks at the book. She decides to keep it. Goes to a drawer, opens it with a key and locks the book away. She exits to the bedroom.

The jangle of keys at the door. IRAJ walks in.

IRAJ. Hello.

SHIDEH (*offstage*). Hi.

SHIDEH returns, she's changed out of her exercise clothes.

Emergency room again?

IRAJ. It's relentless.

SHIDEH heads back into the kitchen. IRAJ takes off his shoes, hangs up his coat. He puts a small plastic bag on the coffee table. SHIDEH returns with a jug of water and tumblers, she sets them onto the dining table.

What's up with you?

SHIDEH. Hungry?

IRAJ. Starving.

SHIDEH. Did you get the yoghurt?

IRAJ. Oh shit.

SHIDEH. Seriously, Iraj?

IRAJ. I'm sorry, I'm sorry.

SHIDEH. I reminded you twice.

IRAJ holds his hands up in surrender.

IRAJ. I know. I'm an idiot.

SHIDEH starts setting the table, laying out the plates and cutlery.

SHIDEH. Don't offer to help if you don't have the time.
I would have just got the yoghurt myself.

SHIDEH *spots a small carrier bag on the coffee table.*

Oh so you remembered to go to the shop. But you forgot the
yoghurt. Honestly, I ask for one thing. One tiny thing.

IRAJ. I said I was sorry.

SHIDEH. What did you buy then? What was so much more
important?

SHIDEH *grabs the bag and looks inside. She gasps.* IRAJ
grins.

Where did you find it?

IRAJ. I got lucky.

SHIDEH. Was it expensive?

IRAJ. Extortionate.

SHIDEH *puts her hand into the plastic bag and pulls out a
single banana. She holds it carefully, as if it is a precious
object.*

SHIDEH. Can I?

SHIDEH *peels the banana. She takes a bite. She savours it.
She takes another. She walks over to* IRAJ, *she breaks off a
piece of banana and feeds it to him. It's delicious.* SHIDEH
*wraps her arms around him affectionately, gives him a kiss
on the cheek.* IRAJ *suddenly snatches the banana from*
SHIDEH *and takes a huge bite.* SHIDEH *laughs, and grabs
it back playfully.*

Hey! Leave some for Dorsa!

DORSA *enters. She runs into* IRAJ*'s arms. He swings her
around.*

DORSA. Baba!

SHIDEH. Come and see what Baba found.

DORSA. Banana!

SHIDEH. Here.

IRAJ. Do you even remember what it tastes like?

DORSA *shrugs, then takes a bite. Her parents watch her intently.* DORSA *chews slowly. Then she spits it out onto the floor.*

DORSA. Yuck. I don't like it.

SHIDEH. DORSA! We don't spit food!

DORSA *sulks.*

IRAJ. It's alright, she just doesn't like it.

SHIDEH. No it's not alright. Food is precious.

SHIDEH *goes off into the kitchen.* IRAJ *kneels down to* DORSA*'s level.*

IRAJ. Dor Dor, go and help your mother.

DORSA *crosses her arms.* IRAJ *gives her a look. She stomps off to the kitchen in a huff.* IRAJ *notices the bin bags full of books, he goes over and looks inside them.* SHIDEH *returns with a cloth, she wipes the banana off the floor.*

What's all this?

SHIDEH *heads back off to the kitchen with the cloth and spat-out banana and returns with a couple of serving dishes of food. Puts them down. Finishes setting the table.*

SHIDEH. Your mother called earlier.

IRAJ. I'll call her back later.

SHIDEH. DORSA? Bring the knives and forks.

IRAJ. Why are all your course books in a bin bag?

SHIDEH. Give them away. Or throw them out.

IRAJ. What happened?

SHIDEH *stops what she's doing. She looks at* IRAJ.

SHIDEH. It's official.

IRAJ. How do you know?

SHIDEH. Mrs Fakur's cousin. But I mean, who were we kidding, it was pretty obvious.

IRAJ. Mrs Fakur's cousin isn't the ultimate authority.

SHIDEH. No. I'm done. It's over.

IRAJ. Oh, Shideh.

SHIDEH. DORSA! I said bring the cutlery.

IRAJ. Hey, hey, come here.

IRAJ tries to hug her, she pushes him away.

SHIDEH. Food's getting cold.

IRAJ. Just stop for one second. Sit down.

SHIDEH stops. She sits on a dining chair.

SHIDEH. I just can't imagine doing anything else. I can't.

IRAJ. I know. I know. But things might get better after the war, hey?

DORSA enters with the knives and forks.

SHIDEH. Sometimes I think, you know, what's the fucking point of anything any more?

DORSA. You said a naughty word.

SHIDEH. Right. Sit down. Time to eat.

SHIDEH takes the knives and forks and sets them on the table.

DORSA. She said a naughty word, Baba.

IRAJ. Adults can say whatever they like. Come here you.

IRAJ jumps up and grabs DORSA playfully, he turns her upside down, pretends she's an aeroplane. She squeals in delight.

SHIDEH. Sit down you two. It's getting cold.

They sit. SHIDEH starts serving the food.

IRAJ. Sleep better last night?

DORSA. No.

SHIDEH. She's been dreaming about planes.

DORSA. It wasn't a dream, I heard them in the sky.

IRAJ. It was probably just the wind.

SHIDEH. That's right. The wind playing tricks.

DORSA. It's okay because now I have this magical furball to
    protect me.

SHIDEH. Not at the table.

IRAJ. What the hell is that?

DORSA. Mehdi gave it to me.

IRAJ. Oh the famous, new Mehdi

DORSA. Mehdi doesn't have a mum and dad.

    A shell fell on their house and Mehdi said his mum's head
    got blown up.

SHIDEH. Oh God.

IRAJ. People exaggerate when they tell stories.

DORSA. Why?

    IRAJ *and* SHIDEH *eat.* DORSA *plays around with the food
    on her plate.*

SHIDEH. Do you want some juice?

DORSA. How did Grandma die?

IRAJ. Dor Dor, not now.

SHIDEH. She was sick.

DORSA. Did it hurt?

SHIDEH. Yes it did.

DORSA. Do you miss her?

SHIDEH. I do.

IRAJ. Dorsa, stop playing with your food and eat your lunch.

DORSA. I'm not hungry.

IRAJ. I almost forgot. I got you a surprise too.

IRAJ stands up and goes to fetch something from his work bag, and holds it behind his back and returns to the table.

DORSA. I already know what it is.

IRAJ. Impossible.

DORSA puts the magic furball to her ear and listens.

SHIDEH. That thing is filthy, Dorsa. Put it away, please.

DORSA. A doll.

IRAJ brings out a doll from behind his back. It's a sort of ragdoll, it wears a dress, with embroidered eyes and smile.

IRAJ. That's just a lucky guess.

DORSA gasps in delight as she embraces the doll.

Next time you're scared, she'll keep you company. What shall we call her?

DORSA thinks for a second.

DORSA. Kimia!

IRAJ. That's a great name. Isn't it Shideh?

SHIDEH. It's a beautiful name for a doll.

IRAJ. Or, I don't know, maybe, a little sister?

SHIDEH stops eating. Gives IRAJ a look.

DORSA. Baba, do you want to hear a joke I made up?

IRAJ. Always.

DORSA. Why was the cow not nice?

IRAJ. I don't know. Why?

DORSA. Because it wasn't in the mooooood.

DORSA and IRAJ giggle together. SHIDEH forces a smile.

IRAJ. Shall we see if we can get Maman to laugh?

SHIDEH. At your jokes? Good luck.

IRAJ. Is that a bet?

SHIDEH *prepares herself, puts on a serious face and looks* IRAJ *in the eyes.*

How many doctors does it take to change a lightbulb?

SHIDEH. How many?

IRAJ. None, they ask the nurse to do it.

SHIDEH *maintains a poker face, rolls her eyes.*

DORSA. I don't get it.

IRAJ. Okay. One more. Why did the communists ban jokes?

SHIDEH. Why?

IRAJ. Because they aren't funny unless everyone gets them.

SHIDEH *can't help smiling.* DORSA *is delighted.*

That's a laugh. I win.

SHIDEH. It was a grin.

DORSA. My turn! My turn! What did the genie say to Aladdin?

IRAJ. I don't know. What?

DORSA. Rub me three times and I'll come.

IRAJ *almost spits out his food.*

SHIDEH. Who told you that joke?

DORSA. No one.

SHIDEH. Dorsa? Tell me right now. Who told you that joke?

DORSA. I made it up.

IRAJ. No you didn't.

DORSA. I did.

IRAJ. Tell us the truth, Dorsa.

SHIDEH. You aren't in trouble, my love.

DORSA. It was Mehdi.

IRAJ. How old is this Mehdi?

DORSA. He's twelve.

SHIDEH. Which means he should know better. I'll be having a
word with Mrs Ebrahimi.

IRAJ. The poor kid just lost both his parents, Shideh.

SHIDEH. She's seven. It's totally inappropriate.

IRAJ. I told worse jokes at his age.

SHIDEH. No. I'm sorry, it's not okay.

IRAJ. And we're late with the rent.

SHIDEH. It doesn't matter.

IRAJ. Fine. Whatever. You're right.

SHIDEH. I know I'm right.

DORSA. Can I go play with Kimia now, Baba?

IRAJ. Sure. Off you go, sweetheart.

DORSA *leaves.* SHIDEH *and* IRAJ *continue eating in
silence.*

SHIDEH. She hadn't finished her lunch.

IRAJ. Her portion's too big.

SHIDEH. No it's not.

IRAJ. It's overwhelming for a small child, all that food.

SHIDEH. Are you a nutritionist now too?

Let's not take it out on each other. Hey?

IRAJ *gets up and stands behind* SHIDEH, *he wraps his arms
around her. Starts massaging her shoulders.*

That feels so good.

IRAJ. You've done everything in your power.

SHIDEH. Don't stop. Keep rubbing.

He continues massaging. SHIDEH *closes her eyes.*

IRAJ. You've been relentless, you've exhausted all avenues, and you said it yourself, maybe it's time to let go.

SHIDEH. I'm so tired of being stuck –

IRAJ. You aren't stuck –

SHIDEH. Every time I see you walk out that door, Iraj. There's this wave of, envy –

IRAJ. I'm sorry.

SHIDEH. It just washes over me, I hate it.

IRAJ. Well, who knows, maybe it's for the best then.

SHIDEH *turns around, shrugs off* IRAJ*'s massage.*

SHIDEH. For the best?

IRAJ. You know what I mean.

SHIDEH. No I don't.

IRAJ. Maybe it's for the best that we all move on.

SHIDEH. We?

IRAJ. As a family. Move forward.

SHIDEH. Move forward?

IRAJ. It would be nice for Dorsa to have a playmate.

SHIDEH. What for?

IRAJ. Well for starters she's lonely, she's always off at the neighbours'.

SHIDEH. She's perfectly happy.

IRAJ. It's not just about her happiness.

SHIDEH. I'm perfectly happy.

IRAJ. Well maybe I want one?

SHIDEH. It's not the right time.

IRAJ. Then when?

A pause.

SHIDEH. What if something changes?

IRAJ. Changes how?

SHIDEH. With the university?

IRAJ. Oh Shideh, come on. You just said you wanted to move on. We've been on hold for years now.

SHIDEH. No. I've been on hold. My career. My life.

IRAJ. There's more to life than work, Shideh. I've been really patient, all these / years I've –

SHIDEH. What if I don't want another child? Full stop.

IRAJ. Well that's a different conversation.

SHIDEH. What's that supposed to mean?

IRAJ. We've always said we'd give her a sibling, and if you've suddenly changed your mind, then that might be a problem for me.

SHIDEH. Have one yourself then.

SHIDEH *starts clearing the table.*

IRAJ. You can't keep putting off this conversation, year after year until it's too late.

SHIDEH. Do we really have to talk about this today? Of all days. Can you just let me grieve. For one day.

SHIDEH *continues to clear the table, brusquely, loudly. She carries plates, cutlery and glasses off into the kitchen. IRAJ settles on the sofa, takes out a few envelopes from his work bag. He sifts through them. SHIDEH returns with a pot of tea and cups, sets it on the table.*

IRAJ. Hey. Come here.

SHIDEH *looks at him, she softens, joins him on the sofa.*

I've been thinking, when I leave on Friday, you and Dorsa should go to my parents.

SHIDEH. We'll be fine here.

IRAJ. It's a whole month. Why stay here all alone? Hey?

SHIDEH. I don't want to be a burden.

IRAJ. It's safer.

SHIDEH. Than where?

IRAJ. Than here, obviously.

SHIDEH. You're the one going to the frontline. Not us.

IRAJ. They're saying Iraq's going to start using missiles, Shideh. They just hit. No siren. No warning.

SHIDEH. Last time we were there your sisters kept saying, 'Tehran gets bombed, and we get the shrapnel.'

IRAJ. They were only joking. You know what they're like.

SHIDEH. All of us squeezed into that little house, with you and your sisters at each other's throats all day long. And me, you and Dorsa, all squashed together on a mattress on the floor for weeks on end. It was unbearable.

IRAJ. I know, I know, but it's just until things calm down.

SHIDEH. The endless housework and cooking, the mindless chatter morning till night –

IRAJ. It's not pleasant, I'll give you that, and I really wish I had a better solution / but –

SHIDEH. The news always on loop, and your father absolutely refusing to put the volume down, chain-smoking in my face all day. I can't. I just can't. I'd lose my mind.

IRAJ. Okay I get it, it's a total nightmare, but it's better than dying!

SHIDEH. Is it?

IRAJ. Oh stop it. You're being / totally unreasonable.

SHIDEH. Last time, when we got back home, we found everything in its place, the whole neighbourhood perfectly serene. We might as well have stayed / right here.

IRAJ. When there is a war on, it's only logical to seek safety.

SHIDEH. So logic dictates that if you're at home we're safe, but as soon as you walk out that door, it's suddenly dangerous. You're not magic, Iraj.

IRAJ. I'm worried about Dorsa.

SHIDEH. What's there to be worried about? She's with me.

IRAJ. You'll be all on your own.

SHIDEH. I ran this household, raised our daughter and nursed my dying mother all by myself, for an entire year, and now you're / worried about Dorsa?

IRAJ. I was here too.

SHIDEH. Barely.

IRAJ. All I'm saying is that I won't be around to support you, at least this way my parents can help, and anyway / they barely get to see her –

SHIDEH. Because you've been really supportive until now. Really hands-on. Pat yourself on the back. Always remembering the little things, like picking up yoghurt.

IRAJ. I got you a banana.

SHIDEH. Fuck your banana.

IRAJ. That's unfair.

SHIDEH. Do you know what's unfair? You swanning off to play doctors and treating me like I'm some / incompetent idiot.

IRAJ. Play doctors? Do you think I enjoy being shipped off to the frontline, Shideh?

SHIDEH *scoffs.*

I don't have a choice! I'd lose the right to practise, then what would we do?

SHIDEH. So if you can't practise it's a catastrophe, but if I can't practise then 'it's for the best'? And 'why don't you just pop out another baby'?

IRAJ. What do you want me to do? Quit in solidarity? Join you on the blacklist? So we all starve?

SHIDEH. You could show a bit more solidarity actually. Yes.

IRAJ. Like how?

SHIDEH. We could move, for example.

IRAJ. Move? Where the hell to?

SHIDEH. Somewhere I'd be allowed to study. Where I could qualify.

IRAJ. Are you suggesting that we, what, just pack up and leave the country?

SHIDEH. I'm only suggesting we go somewhere we can both do our jobs.

IRAJ. Are you seriously suggesting that we abandon everything and everyone we know, uproot our daughter, drag ourselves halfway across the world to some dark, damp European city, where no one even wants us, just so that you can finish your precious studies?

SHIDEH. People do it all the time.

IRAJ. And they never come back.

SHIDEH. It could be a change of scene, an adventure.

IRAJ. Why can't you do something else?

SHIDEH. Like what?

IRAJ. You could be a nurse.

SHIDEH. A nurse?

IRAJ. Don't be such a snob. And anyway, wasn't it your big political ideals that got you into this mess in the first place? I thought you lefties believed all work was equal?

SHIDEH. What kind of future will our daughter have in this country? Huh? Tell me.

IRAJ. Don't play that card.

SHIDEH. Go on. Inspire me.

IRAJ. She'll finish school, then university, and get a job, just like everyone else.

SHIDEH. Until she says the wrong thing? Or thinks for herself? Or her headscarf's too loose?

IRAJ. People adapt. You should try it.

SHIDEH. If I contort myself any further I will fucking break.

IRAJ. We are not moving. End of discussion.

SHIDEH. How can you watch me live like this?

IRAJ. Do you think you're the only person in this country who's suffered?

SHIDEH. At least I put up a fight.

IRAJ. Look how it worked out for you.

SHIDEH. You're spineless

IRAJ. I warned you back then, I told you to be careful. But you never listen. You never listen.

SHIDEH. Why does everything always have to be on your terms?

IRAJ. This is where we live. This is our home. Grow up, move on, and deal with it.

SHIDEH. Thank you for that life-changing advice, I can feel all my problems magically evaporating.

A beat.

All I'm asking is that you meet me in the middle. You owe me.

IRAJ. Owe you? I'm sorry, so it's my fault you can't qualify. It's my fault you wasted all your time on politics at university?

SHIDEH. Do you hear yourself? You sound exactly like them!

IRAJ. You know what? The truth is, if you really wanted to become a doctor then you would have by now.

SHIDEH. That doesn't even make sense.

IRAJ. The universities reopened years ago, why sit around and wait? Why now? Why this sudden urge to return?

SHIDEH. I've been busy raising our child! And now she's at school –

IRAJ. Stop using that excuse. She's been at school for two years.

SHIDEH. It's not an excuse!

IRAJ. You only want to go back now because your mother died.

SHIDEH is stung.

SHIDEH. It's always been my dream to become a doctor.

IRAJ. No Shideh, it's your mother's dream.

SHIDEH's eyes well up.

SHIDEH. Well dead people can't dream.

The lights suddenly go out. A loud hissing noise from the transistor radio fills the room. SHIDEH and IRAJ stare at the radio in fear. Then the red-alert siren screams out. They spring into action. IRAJ scrambles to find a torch. SHIDEH runs off to get DORSA.

IRAJ. Basement. Now.

SHIDEH. DORSA!

SHIDEH returns, pulling DORSA by the hand, she clutches her new doll. DORSA drops Kimia on the floor.

DORSA. Kimia!

IRAJ. Come on! We have to go. NOW!

They rush out of the front door. A moment later, DORSA runs back in. We hear IRAJ calling her name. DORSA rushes to pick the doll up from the floor.

IRAJ *runs in.*

DORSA!

DORSA *grabs Kimia.* IRAJ *picks her up and rushes out of the door.*

Scene Two

Moments later. Basement.

All the residents in the building are squashed together in the basement-come-bomb shelter: SHIDEH, IRAJ, MRS FAKUR, MR EBRAHIMI, MRS EBRAHIMI, PARGOL, MR BIJARI, MEDHI *and* DORSA, *who holds Kimia tightly. It's dark, damp and windowless. A distant rattle of anti-aircraft guns sends ripples of fear through the room.* DORSA *and* MEHDI *hold hands.* SHIDEH *notices, but before she can do anything, a loud rattle shakes the room.*

MRS EBRAHIMI. God damn you, Saddam Hussein. Rot in hell, you bastard.

MRS FAKUR. There's two sides to every war, Mrs Ebrahimi.

MRS EBRAHIMI. To hell with them all then. Is that what you want to hear?

MRS FAKUR. Yes, much better.

MRS EBRAHIMI. So if someone came up and hit you in the face what would you do?

MRS FAKUR. Enough politics.

MRS EBRAHIM. What politics? I'm simply asking what she would do if someone walked up and hit her in the face. Wouldn't you fight back?

MRS FAKUR. Depends who hit me.

MRS EBRAHIMI. A neighbour.

MRS FAKUR. I'd call the police.

MRS EBRAHIMI. Then they'd have a chance to run away. What then?

DORSA. I'd smack them back.

MRS EBRAHIMI. Bravo, Dorsa. Self defence.

SHIDEH. No, Dorsa. We never hit back.

MRS EBRAHIMI. Children are always right, everybody knows the innocent speak the truth.

MRS FAKUR. Fine, so let's say I hit them back. What then? We just hit each other to death. What good is that to anyone?

Louder anti-aircraft gunfire is heard. Everyone jumps. MR BIJARI *yelps in shock.*

PARGOL. It's okay, Baba. It's okay.

MR BIJARI. I'm fine, I'm fine, stop fussing.

MR EBRAHIMI. Don't worry, Mr Bijari, that's the anti-aircraft guns, that's a good sound, means they're shooting at the enemy.

PARGOL. My friend and her whole family packed up and went north yesterday.

MR EBRAHIMI. She's wasting her time, Saddam is just trying to scare us, a few bombs here and there, just to shake us all up a bit.

MRS EBRAHIMI. But if there's one thing he can never shake, it's our morale. Isn't that right?

MR BIJARI. I ran out of morale a very long time ago, Mrs Ebrahimi. My new motto is… What will be, will be.

PARGOL. I heard they've started launching missiles at Tehran.

MR EBRAHIMI. Missiles? Nonsense. That's just hearsay.

IRAJ. I heard that too.

MRS EBRAHIMI. Anyway, missiles or no missiles, the real battle is on the frontlines, not in Tehran, everybody knows that.

MR EBRAHIMI. Exactly.

IRAJ. Well I'd rather be safe than sorry, Mrs Ebrahimi. Shideh and Dorsa are heading north.

MR EBRAHIMI. What about you?

IRAJ. I got my draft notice.

MRS FAKUR. Shideh, you're leaving?

SHIDEH. No. We're just thinking about it.

MR EBRAHIMI. Where are they sending you?

IRAJ. Ilam.

MR EBRAHIMI. Ilam?

MRS EBRAHIMI. God protect you, doctor.

MR EBRAHIMI. My youngest brother is on the front too.

MRS EBRAHIMI *glances over at* MRS FAKUR

MRS EBRAHIMI. Some boys get sent to the front. And some get sent to Paris.

MRS FAKUR. And others get sent to prison and never return.

Everybody is silent.

MR BIJARI. Have I told you my new motto? What / will be will –

PARGOL. You've already said that, Baba.

DORSA. Maman, I'm hungry.

MRS EBRAHIMI. Here Dorsa, come here and have some nuts sweetie. Come come.

DORSA *goes to* MRS EBRAHIMI

I'd give you a drink too, but someone forgot it was their turn to replace the water bottles.

PARGOL. I'm sorry. I've had my hands full.

MRS EBRAHIMI. It's okay. We'll survive. For now.

DORSA *eats her nuts.*

Such a sweet girl. Mehdi, come and eat. Mehdi. MEHDI. God give me patience. Here, give this to the little brat, Dorsa. Good girl.

DORSA takes some nuts to MEHDI.

Pass them around, sweetie. You know if any of us leave Tehran, then we are simply letting Saddam win. We should all stay just to spite him.

PARGOL. I'd rather stay alive, Mrs Ebrahimi.

MRS EBRAHIMI. Anyway it's not so bad down here. Next time we should have a little picnic.

More gunfire is heard.

MR EBRAHIMI. Remember Mr Bijari that's just the sound of victory. Victory!

A very loud explosion. The closest yet. The light flickers and the basement shakes. DORSA yelps and holds onto to SHIDEH. IRAJ automatically shields them both. PARGOL and MR BIJARI cower. Even MRS EBRAHIMI lets out an audible gasp and clutches on to her husband. Only MEHDI remains stoic.

IRAJ. Is everyone okay?

The other respond with reassurances, checking in on each other, etc.

PARGOL. Oh Baba. No, no, no.

DORSA. What's that smell, Maman?

SHIDEH. Quiet, Dorsa. It's nothing.

The smell gets worse. People start to cover their mouths. Someone wretches.

PARGOL. I'm sorry. He can't control himself sometimes. It's not his fault.

IRAJ. No need to be sorry.

MRS EBRAHIMI. Oh my God, I can't breathe.

PARGOL. I'm sorry. If there was a toilet down / here then –

MRS FAKUR. It's okay, Pargol. We're all adults.

DORSA. It stinks.

SHIDEH. Shhh, Dorsa.

MR BIJARI. I'm sorry. I'm so sorry.

An awkward silence.

DORSA. Does anybody want to hear a joke?

SHIDEH. Not now, Dor Dor.

MRS FAKUR. Why not. Cheer us up.

DORSA. Tell them the zombie joke, Mehdi.

MEHDI *shrugs his shoulders and shakes his head no.*

What is it called when zombies have a sleepover?

MRS FAKUR. Hmmm. I don't know.

DORSA. A mass grave.

Scene Three

Two days later. Living room. Nighttime.

SHIDEH *is tidying up* DORSA*'s toys. She finds the magic furball, picks it up, walks over to the bin and throws it away. She spots her course books, still in a black bag. She drags the bag into the living room and starts to return the books to their places on the shelves. Suddenly, the front door slowly creeps open of its own accord.* SHIDEH *turns around. She walks over, peers out into the hallway.*

Nothing. SHIDEH *closes the door, locks the chain, and returns to her books.* IRAJ *enters holding a duffel bag.*

SHIDEH. That was quick.

IRAJ *clocks the empty bin bag and the books returned to their places on the shelves but says nothing.*

IRAJ. She's wiped out.

SHIDEH. Poor kid, spending her childhood hiding in dark basements.

IRAJ. She wouldn't have to do that up north.

SHIDEH *ignores him and returns to her task.*

When there's a war on, people seek shelter, Shideh. For thousands and thousands of years people have sought shelter from wars. We're not special.

SHIDEH. Listen, if it gets bad, I'll pack up and we'll go to your parents. I promise.

IRAJ. You should tape up the windows again.

SHIDEH. Did you leave the rent in the drawer?

IRAJ *puts his jacket on.*

IRAJ. Yes. And the car keys.

A pause.

Will you be alright?

SHIDEH. Will *you* be alright?

IRAJ. I got you something.

SHIDEH. Again? You're spoiling me.

IRAJ. Don't get used to it.

SHIDEH. Where is it?

IRAJ. Pocket.

IRAJ *signals for her to have a look.* SHIDEH *digs around his jacket pockets and pulls out a pot of yoghurt. She wraps her arms around him. They share a long silent hug.*

Well.

SHIDEH. Well.

IRAJ. Goodbye then.

SHIDEH. Right.

IRAJ. Right.

SHIDEH. Call me when you get there.

IRAJ leaves. SHIDEH locks the door and does up the chain. She goes over to the window and watches IRAJ leave, waves him off. She looks around, it suddenly feels empty. She rushes over to some drawers and rummages about for masking tape. She finds it, goes over to the windows and starts to apply masking tape in the shape of an X on each pane.

A power cut. Everything goes dark. SHIDEH gets some candles and lights them. She returns to taping up the windows. Unseen by SHIDEH, DORSA enters silently, she stands very still and watches her mother. SHIDEH finishes the windows and turns around.

DORSA. Why did you put Xs on the window?

SHIDEH sees DORSA and gets a huge fright.

SHIDEH. What are you doing out of bed?

DORSA. I can't find Kimia.

SHIDEH. We'll find her tomorrow, she's probably in your room somewhere.

DORSA. My pyjamas are wet.

SHIDEH. Oh, Dor Dor.

She goes to DORSA, checks her pyjamas, they're soaked.

What did we say about going to the bathroom before bed?

DORSA. Now Baba's not here, can I sleep with you?

SHIDEH. Aren't you a big girl?

DORSA nods.

DORSA. Granny was big and she still wet the bed.

SHIDEH. Remember what I told you? If you wake up and feel you need a pee-pee, you have to get up and go to the bathroom.

DORSA. But I was scared to go to the bathroom without Kimia.

SHIDEH. What's there to be scared of?

DORSA. Djinn.

SHIDEH. Djinn? Djinn aren't real.

DORSA. They are real. We just can't see them.

SHIDEH. Djinn are just silly stories.

DORSA. Mehdi said they're evil and want to hurt us.

SHIDEH. Well Mehdi is talking nonsense.

SHIDEH takes DORSA's hand and tries to move towards the hallway that leads to the bedroom. DORSA resists.

DORSA. Can I watch some cartoons?

SHIDEH. There's no power. So bedtime.

DORSA. Can I tell you about my dream first?

SHIDEH. Okay. But then bed.

DORSA. We were eating our lunch, and the djinn flew in through the window and it ate your head, and then it ate Baba's head. Then you both just sat there with no heads.

SHIDEH. Oh, Dor Dor, that's a horrible dream. But remember it's not real, okay? Dreams are just in our head. Are you gonna sleep with me tonight?

DORSA nods vigorously.

Let's get you cleaned up.

SHIDEH scoops DORSA up in her arms. They walk towards the dark hallway. DORSA clutches on to her mum and whimpers.

Dorsa, you're with me. It's okay.

DORSA. Bring a torch.

SHIDEH goes to a drawer gets the torch and switches it on, DORSA covers her eyes in fear, just as they reach the hallway, the power comes back on, it makes DORSA scream, which makes SHIDEH scream. But there's nothing there. They fall into a fit of giggles.

SHIDEH. Why did you scream?

DORSA. I don't know.

SHIDEH. You almost gave me a heart attack.

DORSA. Can I watch cartoons now?

SHIDEH. Nice try. It's bedtime for you, pee-pee pants.

They exit to the bedroom.

Scene Four

The next morning.

The radio in the living room suddenly bursts into life, static turns into the sound of a tannoy playing war propaganda music. We are at the offices of the Student Selection Committee at the University of Tehran. A couple of female STUDENTS enter and sit on a row of chairs, they wear black headscarves and robes. SHIDEH enters wearing a loose headscarf, she sits on a chair, she fiddles with her headscarf nervously. A SECRETARY enters, leafing through some documents. SHIDEH jumps up.

SHIDEH. Excuse me?

SECRETARY. Yes?

SHIDEH. It's just I've been waiting for hours.

SECRETARY. And?

SHIDEH. Do you know how long it might be? I've left my
   daughter with my neighbour and I need –

SECRETARY. Do you have an appointment?

SHIDEH. No, but I need to speak to the committee director
   quite urgently.

SECRETARY. He's very busy today.

SHIDEH. I only need two minutes of his time.

SECRETARY. Hundreds of students only need two of minutes of his time. It adds up.

SHIDEH. Well then just one minute, even half a minute.

SECRETARY. I already told you he's busy right now.

SHIDEH. Then I'll wait.

SECRETRY. You'll be waiting all day. You're better off coming back very early tomorrow.

SHIDEH. What time?

SECRETARY. Early.

SHIDEH. Can I make an appointment?

SECRETARY. What's your name?

SHIDEH *hesitates.*

If you don't give me your name I can't help you.

SHIDEH *hands over her identification papers.*

SHIDEH. Shideh Bozorgmehr.

SECRETARY. Wait here.

The SECRETARY *exits.* SHIDEH *waits nervously for a few minutes. The* SECRETARY *returns.*

I suggest you go home, Mrs Bozorgmehr.

SHIDEH. Why?

SECRETARY. Because the committee director is busy for the rest of the week.

SHIDEH. You just said I should try tomorrow morning.

SECRETARY. That was before I checked his schedule.

SHIDEH. I can come back next week.

SECRETARY. His schedule is also full next week.

SHIDEH. Then I'll come back the week after.

SECRETARY. I imagine he's busy that week too.

SHIDEH. In that case I'll come back every day and every week
until he sees me.

SECRETARY. God willing.

Scene Five

Later that day, afternoon. The apartment.

MRS EBRAHIMI *stands at the front door with* DORSA *who
is clutching Kimia.* SHIDEH *is in the middle of taking off her
headscarf and shoes.*

DORSA. Look, Maman, we found her!

SHIDEH. She's been looking for that doll everywhere, thank
you so much, Mrs Ebrahimi. Say thank you, Dorsa.

DORSA. Thank you, Mrs Ebrahimi.

DORSA *runs off and exits to her bedroom.*

MRS EBRAHIMI. She's such a sweet girl.

SHIDEH. Thank you for finding her doll, she won't sleep
without it at the moment.

MRS EBRAHIMI. I found it in Mehdi's room, I'm so sorry Mrs
Bozorgmehr.

SHIDEH. He was probably just keeping it safe for her.

MRS EBRAHIMI. What does a big boy like him want with a
little girl's doll?

SHIDEH. Please come in.

MRS EBRAHIMI. Oh no I can't, I've got to get lunch ready.

SHIDEH. Actually, Mrs Ebrahimi, I wanted to talk to you about
something.

MRS EBRAHIMI. Oh. Nothing serious I hope?

SHIDEH. No no, it's just about the kids. Come in.

MRS EBRAHIMI *comes in,* SHIDEH *leads her to the sofa.*

Would you like some tea?

MRS EBRAHIMI. Oh no, thank you.

SHIDEH. Just a cup.

MRS EBRAHIMI. I'm fine.

SHIDEH. I insist.

MRS EBRAHIMI. I can't stay long.

SHIDEH *exits to the kitchen and returns with a glass of water and a small plate of nuts and dried fruit, she sets it on the table in front of* MRS EBRAHIMI.

SHIDEH. It's about Mehdi.

MRS EBRAHIMI. What has that little devil done now?

SHIDEH. Oh nothing, he's been telling Dorsa scary stories, I'm sure he doesn't mean to frighten her, but she's been having nightmares and she's not sleeping, and I'm exhausted, so if you could just talk to him –

MRS EBRAHIMI. Your daughter must be confused.

SHIDEH. Why would she be confused?

MRS EBRAHIMI. Because Mehdi is mute.

SHIDEH *is taken aback.*

Not a word since he lost his parents. They were both killed right in front of his eyes in an air raid. Can you believe it?

SHIDEH. Poor little thing.

MRS EBRAHIMI. Ebrahimi's taken him to every doctor in town, I've tried all the cures, I even gave him raw dove eggs – I had to steal them from the neighbour's garden. But nothing. Not a peep to anyone.

SHIDEH. But Dorsa said that Mehdi told her these stories –

MRS EBRAHIMI. What kind of stories?

SHIDEH. I don't know, fairy tales, djinn, that kind of
    nonsense –

MRS EBRAHIMI. Djinn? God have mercy.

    MRS EBRAHIMI *fearfully starts to recite a prayer.*

SHIDEH. Djinn aren't real.

MRS EBRAHIMI. There's an entire surah in the Quran named
    after them, and you think they aren't real?

SHIDEH. If you could just speak to Mehdi and –

MRS EBRAHIMI. Between you and me, my husband gets
    angry when I say this, but that boy scares me, and the truth
    is, I don't want him around when this baby is born.

SHIDEH. He's been through a terrible shock. He's grieving.

MRS EBRAHIMI. I had my doubts, but now? Now I'm sure.
    He's going around terrorising a little girl, stealing her doll,
    and talking about djinn? God help us.

SHIDEH. I really don't want to get him into trouble.

MRS EBRAHIMI. You know I'm not the kind of person who
    gossips about her own relatives, but the other day –

    MRS EBRAHIMI *looks around to see no one is listening.*
    She lowers her voice.

    I saw him whispering to a cat.

SHIDEH. He was probably just playing.

MRS EBRAHIMI. And sometimes, I catch that boy just
    standing there staring at nothing, always at empty corners, or
    up at the ceiling. These are all signs, Mrs Bozorghmer.

SHIDEH. Signs of what?

    She checks the coast is clear.

MRS EBRAHIMI. That he might be possessed. Or halfway
    there. What kind of djinn did he tell Dorsa about?

SHIDEH. I don't believe in djinn, Mrs Ebrahimi.

MRS EBRAHIMI. Whether you believe in them or not Mrs Bozorgmehr, I'm telling you, something's not right. I can feel it. And it's not just Mehdi, everyone in this building is all out of sorts, don't you think?

SHIDEH. We're all under a lot of / stress, so –

MRS EBRAHIMI. My husband has been having terrible nightmares, even sleepwalking. And yesterday – (*She checks the coast is clear.*) I heard Pargol crying on the stairs, whispering to herself. And then there's the wind –

SHIDEH. If you could please talk to Mehdi.

MRS EBRAHIMI. Oh I will, don't you worry about that. And Mrs Bozorghmehr? Be vigilant.

DORSA *enters and runs up to the women.*

DORSA. Maman can I watch my video, please?

MRS EBRAHIMI*'s ears prick up at the word 'video'.*

SHIDEH. What video? Stop being silly and go and play with your toys.

DORSA *is confused. She stomps off and opens her toybox, starts setting up a plastic tea party set and a little circle of stuffed animals.*

MRS EBRAHIMI. Is that the time? I better be going.

SHIDEH. Thank you so much for watching her and for finding her doll, Mrs Ebrahimi.

MRS EBRAHIMI. No trouble at all. Anytime.

MRS EBRAHIMI *leaves.* SHIDEH *escorts her to the door.*

SHIDEH. Dorsa? You know you aren't allowed to talk about our videos in front of people.

DORSA *doesn't respond, she's absorbed in her game.* SHIDEH *takes the tray into the kitchen. She returns.*

We could get into trouble. Do you understand, my love?

DORSA continues playing and ignores her mother. SHIDEH lies down on the sofa. She closes her eyes.

DORSA. Kimia wants to have a tea party with you.

SHIDEH. I just want to close my eyes for ten minutes, okay?

DORSA. Why? You haven't done anything today.

SHIDEH. What have you done today?

DORSA. You don't go to work like Baba.

SHIDEH. I look after you, after the house. That's work.

DORSA. That's just tidying up.

SHIDEH closes her eyes again and tries to ignore DORSA.

How many sleeps till Baba comes back?

SHIDEH. A lot.

DORSA. You never play with me any more.

SHIDEH. I'll play with you in a minute.

DORSA sulks and stomps off to her bedroom. The doorbell rings. SHIDEH groans.

What now?

SHIDEH reluctantly drags herself off the sofa and opens the door, clearly irritated. PARGOL stands there with an empty glass in her hand.

PARGOL. Were you sleeping?

SHIDEH. No no. Wide awake. Come in.

PARGOL steps inside. She holds out the glass.

PARGOL. I was the middle of making a cake. Ran out of sugar. Could I trouble you?

SHIDEH smiles, takes the glass.

SHIDEH. Do you want some tea?

PARGOL. My father's all alone upstairs. Maybe next time.

SHIDEH *heads off to the kitchen with the empty glass. She returns moments later with the glass, now brim-full of sugar and hands it to* PARGOL. PARGOL *keeps hold of* SHIDEH*'s hand for a moment too long.*

How did you do it?

SHIDEH. Do what?

PARGOL. All that time with your mother?

SHIDEH. It wasn't easy.

PARGOL. How did you not lose it?

SHIDEH. Oh, Pargol. Of course I lost it. Come on, let's have some tea. It's been a while.

PARGOL. I shouldn't.

SHIDEH. How is your dad?

PARGOL. He can't dress himself any more, he refuses to eat half the time, one day his memory is as sharp as anything, and the next he confuses me for my mother. Now all this talk about missiles, I'm desperate to go north, but he won't listen. Anything I say, he says the opposite, just to spite me. Maybe you could talk to him, Shideh?

SHIDEH. Me?

PARGOL. He likes you. He'll listen to you.

SHIDEH. It's really not my place, Pargol.

PARGOL. Please, Shideh, I wouldn't ask if I wasn't desperate. I don't have a sister, or a mother, it's just me, and he won't listen. He just won't listen. Will you talk to him?

SHIDEH. Pargol.

PAGOL. Won't you help me?

SHIDEH. Okay. I'll give it a try.

PARGOL *hugs* SHIDEH *in gratitude.* DORSA *runs in, she spots* PARGOL *and runs straight into her arms.*

PARGOL. Dorsa!

DORSA. Will you play tea parties with me?

PARGOL. I wish I could, sweetheart, but I'm busy baking a cake. Shall I bring you a piece when it's ready?

DORSA *nods enthusiastically.* PARGOL *pinches* DORSA*'s cheek.*

Thank you, Shideh. Thank you.

PARGOL *exits.*

DORSA. You never bake cakes.

SHIDEH. Shall we have that tea party then?

DORSA. Really?

DORSA *is thrilled, she hugs* SHIDEH *and then takes her by the hand to the tea party she's set up.*

SHIDEH. Oh wow, look at all your guests, you're very popular. What's the occasion?

DORSA. It's Kimia's birthday.

SHIDEH. You should have told me, I haven't brought her a present!

DORSA. It's okay, she's just really happy you're here.

SHIDEH. Well I'm honoured to be invited. What's on the menu?

DORSA. Do you like strawberry tea?

SHIDEH. I love strawberry tea.

DORSA *pours* SHIDEH *some tea, then fills ups the other cups.* SHIDEH *sips hers.*

DORSA. Would you like a biscuit?

SHIDEH. Yes please. Oh, thank you.

DORSA *serves* SHIDEH *an imaginary biscuit.* SHIDEH *eats it.*

This is delicious. It's the best biscuit in the whole of Iran.

DORSA. It's worm flavour.

SHIDEH. Oh, I love worms. How did you know they were my favourite?

DORSA. I also have spider biscuits, and cockroach biscuits and fart biscuits.

SHIDEH. Give me one of your cockroach biscuits please. I hope they're nice and crunchy?

DORSA giggles and serves an imaginary cockroach biscuit. SHIDEH tucks in.

Oh hold on, there's a cockroach leg stuck in my teeth.

SHIDEH picks the cockroach leg out of her teeth and flicks it at DORSA.

DORSA. Yuck!

SHIDEH. Could I have some more tea, please? And another of your delicious biscuits. I'll try the fart flavour.

DORSA excitedly gets the teapot and fills up SHIDEH's cup before topping up the others.

Dor Dor? You know the stories that you said Mehdi told you?

DORSA. Sometimes we both tell stories.

DORSA serves SHIDEH her biscuit.

SHIDEH. Thank you. Mrs Ebrahimi told me that Mehdi, well, she said he doesn't speak very much. Or at all, actually.

DORSA. He whispers things in my ear.

SHIDEH. Like what?

DORSA. Like. Be careful.

SHIDEH. Why be careful?

DORSA hesitates. She looks at SHIDEH, scared to tell her.

DORSA. Because they're coming.

A pause. DORSA stares up at the ceiling, and for a moment, it's as if she's starting to go into a trance. The phone rings. It makes them both jump. SHIDEH goes to pick it up.

SHIDEH. Hello? Iraj?

The line's cutting up. Hello?

…

We miss you too. How is it over there?

…

Sounds awful.

…

No. We're fine here, honestly it's been so quiet.

…

DORSA. Maman we haven't finished the tea party.

SHIDEH *signals for* DORSA *to be quiet.*

SHIDEH. Those are just rumours, Iraj.

…

What missiles?

…

I'm not abandoning my home based on a rumour.

…

Dorsa's better off here. Hello?

Sounds can be heart faintly from the receiver, loud bangs and then shouting.

Iraj? What was that sound? IRAJ?

The line goes dead, faint sound of the dial tone.

Hello? Iraj? Can you hear me? Iraj? Are you there? Hello?

SHIDEH *reluctantly hangs up.*

DORSA. Maman?

SHIDEH *rushes over to a shelf and grabs the transistor radio and tries to tune into the BBC Persian service, she catches the signal for a few seconds.*

Maman? Is Baba okay?

SHIDEH. Just hold on, Dorsa.

SHIDEH *loses the signal from the radio, tries to move to a better spot,* DORSA *follows her. The radio signal returns,* JANE FONDA*'s voice from the workout tape comes through,* SHIDEH *is totally perplexed.*

JANE FONDA. *And back six seven eight and now jog in place again, one two three four five, start to slow it down, stand still, slowly roll down, put your arms out for a tendon stretch, to the right, four counts –*

DORSA. Your fart biscuit has gone stale. MAMAN!

SHIDEH. Playtime's over now, my love.

JANE FONDA*'s voice disappears into static.* SHIDEH *moves around trying to catch the signal.* DORSA *comes over and starts to shove Kimia in her mother's face.*

DORSA. It's not over. It's not. It's not. It's not.

SHIDEH. Dorsa, STOP IT.

The radio tunes back in to the BBC Persian service. There's heavy static, in between snatches of a news bulletin, the words 'missile attack' and 'Tehran' can just about be made out. SHIDEH *tries to concentrate.* DORSA *shoves the doll into* SHIDEH*'s face again.*

Dorsa, stop that. This is important.

DORSA *doesn't stop. She keeps shoving Kimia in* SHIDEH*'s face.*

I said stop. NOW.

SHIDEH *loses the radio signal. Suddenly,* SHIDEH *grabs Kimia and throws the doll across the room.* DORSA *is shocked.*

When I say playtime is over, it means it's over. And the next time you don't do as you're told, I'll take Kimia away and you'll never see her again. Understood?

DORSA *starts to cry. She runs off to grab Kimia and cradles her. She glares at* SHIDEH.

DORSA. Mehdi was right about you.

You're dangerous.

SHIDEH. What did you say?

DORSA. You hurt Kimia.

DORSA gets up and walks over to the TV, she pulls out the box of videotapes, takes the Jane Fonda cassette and raises her arm as if to throw it across the room. Her arm hovers.

SHIDEH. Don't you dare.

The radio bursts into life, the red-alert siren screams out of into the apartment.

Scene Six

The basement.

SHIDEH *and* DORSA, MRS FAKUR, MR EBRAHIMI, MRS EBRAHIMI *and* MEHDI, PARGOL *and* MR BIJARI *are all huddled together.* MEHDI *and* DORSA *play together silently.* DORSA *whispers into* MEHDI's *ear.* SHIDEH *watches them carefully.* MRS FAKUR *is reading a novel,* La Peste *by Albert Camus.* SHIDEH *and* MRS FAKUR *speak in whispers together.* MRS EBRAHIMI *is desperate to eavesdrop.*

MRS EBRAHIMI. What's the news from Ilam, Mrs Bozorgmehr? How is the doctor?

SHIDEH. He's fine.

MRS EBRAHIMI. I heard it's very very bad down there. God protect him.

SHIDEH. Thank you.

MRS EBRAHIMI. When we win the war, it will all be worth it.

MRS FAKUR. Nobody wins wars. Everybody loses.

MRS FAKUR goes back to her novel.

PARGOL. I couldn't agree more, Mrs Fakur.

The sound of shelling feels closer. Everybody listens. Then, a big one. The basement shakes a little. Some gasps, grabbing on to each other.

No sign of those anti-aircraft guns tonight is there, Mr Ebrahimi?

MR EBRAHIMI. They aren't fireworks. The army use them strategically, tactically.

PARGOL. If it was up to me, I'd leave Tehran first thing tomorrow, my cousin says we can stay with him, but my father here won't listen.

PARGOL *shoots* SHIDEH *a look, or a nudge.*

MR BIJARI. Oh don't start with your nagging in front of everyone.

PARGOL. He says if he's forced to leave his home he might as well go back to his own village.

MR EBRAHIMI. In Kurdistan? Are you out of your mind? It's a disaster there.

MR BIJARI. Exactly. Which is why we should stay right here in Tehran.

Another explosion. Louder.

PARGOL. Can't you hear that? Can't you all hear that? Or is it just me?

MR EBRAHIMI. It wasn't very close. The sound carries.

MR BIJARI. Do you hear that Pargol? The sound carries.

PARGOL. Someone make him see sense, I beg you. I'm losing my mind. I can't breath down here. What are we still doing here?

MR BIJARI. I don't want to leave my home and live with strangers, all packed together like sardines.

PARGOL. They're not strangers, they're family.

MR BIJARI. We barely know them.

PARGOL. Shideh, talk to him please.

MR BIJARI. I'm almost eighty years old, I'm staying right here in my home, where I belong.

PARGOL. Shideh, say something!

SHIDEH *hesitates.*

MRS EBRAHIMI. That's the spirit, Mr Bijari. If we leave, we might as well be waving a big white flag. They win.

PARGOL. They'll definitely win when a missile drops on our heads and buries us all under the rubble.

MR BIJARI. My wife, the eternal optimist!

PARGOL. No Baba, it's me, Pargol.

MR EBRAHIMI. Don't lose hope. Whatever you do.

PARGOL. Hope? Look around you. The whole world is standing behind them. America, Europe, the Arabs.

MR EBRAHIMI. Who cares.

PARGOL. I care. Who's on our side? Tell me.

MR EBRAHIMI. You're right. We're all alone in this world. The army's at its limits. And look at us all, hiding down here in the dark. But me? I fear nothing. Ask me why.

PARGOL. Why?

MR EBRAHIMI. I submit myself to God's will. Because everything is already written.

MR BIJARI. And what will be, will be.

More shelling is heard in the distance. Another explosion close by.

PARGOL. You're all mad. Every single one of you.

SHIDEH *tries to comfort* PARGOL, *but she brushes her off.*

MRS EBRAHIMI. What are you reading, Mrs Fakur?

MRS FAKUR. A novel.

MRS EBRAHIMI. I wish I had time for stories. Between Mehdi and the house and the tiredness from this baby, I barely have time to do my prayers. Why don't you read us some of your story Mrs Fakur, so we don't all die of boredom?

MRS FAKUR. It's in French

MR EBRAHIMI. Don't you have any books in Farsi?

MRS FAKUR. I do. Many. But this one is in French.

MRS EBRAHIMI. What a shame. If it was in Farsi then we could have all enjoyed a story.

DORSA. Are we having a story?

MRS EBRAHIMI. Only if you speak French, sweetheart.

MR BIJARI *leans in and addresses* DORSA.

MR BIJARI. I can tell you a story Pargol joon.

PARGOL *goes to correct him but is stopped by* MRS FAKUR. MR BIJARI *tells his story, everyone gradually leans further in, until they are all huddled around him.*

When I was a little boy, about your age, I lived in a village. There were only a handful of houses back then, and there was this one old house right at the end of an alley, it must have been over two hundred years old, it was dark and gloomy and the wooden shutters were all rotten. There was an old lady who lived there all alone, and she was very strange, kept herself to herself, always wore black, from head to toe, and no one had ever seen her smile. Once, my brother swore he'd seen her eating soil in her garden, shovelling clumps of dirt into her mouth. People said she was a djinn, a wolfwoman, and that she kidnapped children and ate them for dinner. All of us kids were terrified of her and one summer when the days were endless and we'd run out of games to play, we dared each other to run up and knock on her door. The first boy, the bravest of us all, walked up on his tiptoes, silently. He knocked once and ran away like the wind. We watched. We waited. Nothing. The next boy did the same. We waited. Nothing. And then it was my turn. I walked up to the house, my knees knocking together, my stomach churning. And just as I put my hand up to knock, the door creaks open, all by itself, the first thing I see are her feet, well they weren't feet, they were hairy, with sharp claws, and I slowly look up at the rest of her, and there she was, half wolf, half human, feasting on a little boy.

DORSA. I'm scared.

SHIDEH. Don't worry, Dor Dor, it's only a story.

MR BIJARI. Oh no, it's true. Every word.

MRS EBRAHIMI. God save us all.

Scene Seven

The next morning. The apartment.

The curtains are closed, shutting out the daylight. SHIDEH *is doing her Jane Fonda video. She's in full swing.* DORSA *enters in her pyjamas, clutching Kimia. She silently walks across to the dining table, sits down, and glares at* SHIDEH.

SHIDEH. Good morning

DORSA *doesn't answer.*

I said good morning, Dorsa.

The workout video comes to an end. SHIDEH *walks over to the TV, switches it off and puts the video and machine away. She walks over to* DORSA, *tries to stroke her hair.* DORSA *pulls away.*

Someone's still grumpy. Do you want some juice?

DORSA *shrugs. The doorbell rings.*

SHIDEH *walks to the front door and opens it. It's* MEHDI.

Oh Mehdi. Hello.

MEHDI *walks in. He stares at* SHIDEH. DORSA *runs towards him, pushing past* SHIDEH.

DORSA. MEHDI!

DORSA *hugs* MEHDI *and pulls him inside,*

Can Mehdi stay and play?

SHIDEH. Mehdi, does your aunt know you're here?

MEHDI *nods.* DORSA *grabs his hand and they run into the living room and sit down where* DORSA*'s toys are spread out.*

Stay out here in the living room. Dorsa? Did you hear what I said?

DORSA *ignores* SHIDEH *and plays with* MEHDI.

I'll make you some breakfast then shall I? Since you're being so polite.

SHIDEH *goes off to the kitchen. The children play silently. Then* MEHDI *stands up and looks up at the ceiling. He stares.* DORSA *copies him.*

MEHDI *exits to the corridor that leads to the bedrooms, he beckons* DORSA *to follow him. They exit. A few moments later,* SHIDEH *enters from the kitchen with a tray of toast, oranges and two glasses of orange juice.*

Dorsa? Mehdi?

SHIDEH *puts the tray down. She checks under the table. Then behind the sofa.*

She hears a noise coming from the bedrooms, and exits through the corridor. Moments later, SHIDEH *enters, with* MEHDI *and* DORSA *marching ahead of her, looking sheepish.* DORSA *is wearing an adult-sized chador.*

What were you doing in my bedroom? Take that off. You know you aren't supposed to touch my things, Dorsa.

SHIDEH *takes the chador off* DORSA.

I asked you a question. Both of you.

DORSA. We were just playing families.

SHIDEH. I'm afraid playtime's over now, Mehdi. Dorsa, go and sit at the table.

DORSA *stamps her feet and marches over to the dining table. She sits down and crosses her arms with a sulk.* SHIDEH *walks* MEHDI *to the door.*

You can come and play another day, Mehdi. Okay?

MEHDI *exits.* SHIDEH *takes the chador to the coat rack and hangs it up.*

What were you doing with Mehdi in the bedroom, Dorsa?

DORSA. We were playing families.

SHIDEH. What does that mean?

DORSA. It means I made the breakfast and he went to work.

SHIDEH. Dorsa, when I give you an instruction, it's only because I want you to be safe. Do you understand?

DORSA *nods.*

Here, have some orange.

DORSA. Oranges are stupid.

SHIDEH. Dor Dor, I'm sorry about before, when I shouted and threw Kimia.

SHIDEH *gives* DORSA *a kiss, strokes her hair.* DORSA *lets her.*

DORSA. Say sorry to Kimia.

SHIDEH. Sorry, Kimia.

DORSA. Did Baba call?

SHIDEH. He did. He sends you a big kiss. And he said to make sure Dorsa eats more fruit.

DORSA. If I eat some orange can I watch my Michael Jackson video?

SHIDEH. Yes.

DORSA *stuffs her mouth with some pieces of orange and runs over and jumps on the sofa. She leaves Kimia on the kitchen table.* SHIDEH *goes over to the TV and finds* DORSA*'s tape. She puts in on, it's Michael Jackson's 'Thriller' music video.* DORSA *watches her video and* SHIDEH *starts to clear up the breakfast stuff from the table.*

There's a loud explosion in the near distance. The apartment shakes ever so slightly. Another one. Even closer.

Oh my God.

DORSA *stops watching TV and looks up at the ceiling.*

And then the inevitable devastating sound of impact.

Everything goes black.

For a few seconds there is an eerie silence, as if the world is on mute.

The panel above the apartment rises to reveal the Bijaris' living room to the audience. A huge, unexploded missile has crashed straight into the floor of the apartment on the floor above. It looks as if it's crashed through the roof of the theatre.

The silence is broken by SHIDEH*'s screaming. She calls out for* DORSA, *she tries to find her in the dark. We can hear her stumbling around, trying to reach the window.*

DORSA? DORSA?

SHIDEH *finds the window and opens the curtains, daylight streams in and reveals the room is enveloped in dust, plaster falls from the ceiling, objects thrown across the floor.* DORSA *is nowhere to be seen.* SHIDEH *searches for her frantically. She finally spots* DORSA *standing frozen in place, staring up at the ceiling, covered in dust. She looks like an apparition. Kimia is gone from the dining table.*

Oh Dorsa!

SHIDEH *throws her arms around* DORSA, *who remains frozen, statuelike.* SHIDEH *frantically checks her over for injuries.*

Oh God. Oh God. Dorsa. Let me look at you. Let me see. Are you okay? Does anything hurt?

SHIDEH *grabs* DORSA *and tries to pull her away towards the door, but* DORSA *won't budge. She stands stiff and continues to stare up at the ceiling, almost possessed.*

We have to go downstairs.

DORSA. I saw them.

SHIDEH *pulls* DORSA *by the arms.*

They're here. I saw them.

SHIDEH *tries to pick up* DORSA *but she resists.*

SHIDEH. We have to go!

DORSA. No!

MR EBRAHIMI *bursts in, desperately dragging an unconscious* MR BIJARI, MRS EBRAHIMI *struggles to help him. They are followed by* PARGOL, *who is in hysterics.* MRS FAKUR *follows close behind with* MEHDI. *The missile sits ominously over the commotion.*

PARGOL. Help him! Help him, Shideh, please!

MRS EBRAHIMI. There was no siren, no warning, nothing.

PARGOL. Shideh, I'm begging you, help him.

SHIDEH *and* MR EBRAHIMI *place* MR BIJARI *on the floor.* SHIDEH *checks his pulse and breathing.* MEHDI *stares up at the missile silently, eyes wide.*

MR EBRAHIMI. Someone call an ambulance.

PARGOL. He's dying, Shideh, help him.

MRS FAKUR. Dorsa, come here, come downstairs with me.

MRS FAKUR *goes over to* DORSA *and takes her hand, but she won't move from* SHIDEH'*s side.* MR EBRAHIMI *finds a cushion for* MR BIJARI'*s head.*

SHIDEH. Dorsa, go with Mrs Fakur.

PARGOL. Please please, help him.

MRS FAKUR *grabs* DORSA *and starts to drag her away. She kicks and screams for her mum.*

SHIDEH. Dorsa, do as you're told!

DORSA. They're here. I saw them. They're here!

MRS FAKUR manages to drag DORSA out of the apartment kicking and screaming. They exit along with MEHDI. MRS EBRAHIMI watches helplessly.

PARGOL. Save him, Shideh, you're a doctor

SHIDEH. I'm not a real doctor, Pargol.

PARGOL. Do something please. Oh Baba. My Baba.

SHIDEH. Okay. Okay. Give me some space.

MR EBHRAHIMI. We should take him downstairs. Drive him to a hospital.

SHIDEH. We can't, he won't make it.

MRS EBRAHIMI. That thing hasn't exploded, it could blow up any minute.

SHIDEH. No. I need to start CPR right now or he'll die.

SHIDEH starts to do chest compressions on MR BIJARI.

MR EBRAHIMI. What are you doing?

PARGOL. Please save him. You're a doctor, Shideh.

SHIDEH. I'm trying.

SHIDEH continues the chest compressions.

Come on. Come on. Come on.

MR EBRAHIMI. We need get him to a hospital.

PARGOL. Baba, it's okay. I'm here. I'm right here, Baba.

SHIDEH continues. MR EBRAHIMI watches helplessly.

It's going to be okay. Isn't it, Shideh?

SHIDEH continues for a while. PARGOL whimpers quietly and holds her dad's hand, cradles his head.

SHIDEH continues doing chest compressions in silence. It's clearly over, but she carries on anyway. Eventually, reluctantly, she stops.

What are you doing? Don't stop.

SHIDEH. I'm sorry, Pargol. I'm so sorry.

PARGOL. What? No. No. No.

SHIDEH. There's nothing more we can do.

PARGOL. Try again. Try again, Shideh, please.

SHIDEH. I'm sorry.

PARGOL. I beg you. Don't stop. Don't stop.

SHIDEH *holds* PARGOL. MR EBRAHIMI *grabs a blanket from the sofa and covers* MR BIJARI*'s body. He exits.* PARGOL *weeps in* SHIDEH*'s arms.*

He hadn't eaten his breakfast, Shideh.

He died with an empty stomach. They took him before he'd had a bite to eat.

I let him die hungry.

Don't leave me all alone. I beg you Baba.

I beg you.

I beg you.

SHIDEH *holds* PARGOL, *she embraces her, she rocks back and forth with her in her grief. Eventually two* PARAMEDICS *come in and take* MR BIJARI *away.* MRS EBRAHIMI *gently escorts* PARGOL *out.* SHIDEH *sits in the wreckage. Stunned and silent.*

Nighttime descends. Some plaster and dust crumbles from a crack in the ceiling above her head. Suddenly, a gentle gust of wind blows into the apartment. The curtains billow. SHIDEH *shivers. She goes over to the window. She goes to close it but finds it's firmly shut. The curtains go still. Footsteps sound from upstairs,* SHIDEH *looks up. Then the television comes on all by itself.* SHIDEH *freezes. Then she slowly walks over to the TV and turns it off.*

Scene Eight

The next day. Evening.

SHIDEH *and* MRS FAKUR *stand in the aftermath. The sheet that has been covering* MR BIJARI *still lies on the floor.* MRS FAKUR *holds a broom, ready to clean up.*

MRS FAKUR. This place looks like it's been hit by a bomb.

> MRS FAKUR *picks something up from the floor.*

> Where does this go?

> SHIDEH *motions to a cabinet.*

> Where are your bin bags?

> SHIDEH *motions to the kitchen.* MRS FAKUR *exits.* SHIDEH *picks up the blanket.*

> MRS FAKUR *returns with the binbags.*

SHIDEH. My hands feel strange.

> MRS FAKUR *opens a bin bag,* SHIDEH *puts the blanket in the bag.*

> I should have listened, taken him downstairs, got him to a hospital.

MRS FAKUR. You were very brave yesterday, Shideh.

SHIDEH. He might have made it.

MRS FAKUR. He wouldn't have made it to the bottom of the stairs.

SHIDEH. Mrs Fakur? I think I counted wrong.

> MRS FAKUR *goes over to* SHIDEH.

> I panicked, my mind went blank, because I'm not a doctor, am I?

MRS FAKUR. You've had a big shock.

SHIDEH. I felt his heart stop, the last beat, right here in the palm of my hand.

MRS FAKUR guides SHIDEH *to the sofa.*

MRS FAKUR. We've all had a big shock. Sit down.

SHIDEH *finally sits on the sofa, she puts her head in her hands.* MRS FAKUR *gets an idea.*

I know what we need to lift our spirits.

MRS FAKUR *exits to the kitchen.*

(*Offstage*). Found it!

She returns with a bottle of moonshine and two glasses. She puts the bottle down and pours two glasses.

Here you go. Drink up.

They drink. It hits the spot.

SHIDEH. If I tell you something, will you promise not to – no, forget it.

MRS FAKUR. Well, you have to tell me now!

SHIDEH. No, you'll just laugh at me.

MRS FAKUR. When have I ever laughed at you, Shideh? Here, another drop, for courage.

MRS FAKUR *tops up their glasses.*

SHIDEH. I think there might be something in the apartment.

MRS FAKUR. What something?

SHIDEH. I don't know. A djinn.

MRS FAKUR *bursts out laughing.*

You said you wouldn't laugh. I'm serious.

MRS FAKUR. Oh you're serious, are you? Djiin? Come on, Shideh, you are the most rational person I know, don't be so ridiculous.

SHIDEH. You're the one that has an evil eye hanging over her door.

MRS FAKUR. That's just aesthetics.

SHIDEH. Things have been moving, the curtains, the TV / and Dorsa –

MRS FAKUR. If your mother was here, God rest her soul, she would have smacked you across the head.

SHIDEH. I don't know, at the end, she'd ramble on and on about being cursed, beg me to burn esfand. I even heard her praying.

She's been in my dreams this week. I don't know why.

MRS FAKUR. My mother died over thirty years ago, and even today, very occasionally, at the supermarket, for a split second, I think I glimpse her green skirt, brushing past me, or out of nowhere, I catch the smell of her hands, orange peel and sugared almonds.

And sometimes. I hear her whispering in my ear, it's her voice, I'd never forget it, and she says…

'Have another drink.'

MRS FAKUR *tops them up.*

SHIDEH. What would I do without you?

MRS FAKUR. My son called me three times this morning. A friend rang him up, told him about that damned missile. Can't keep anything private these days.

SHIDEH. How is he?

MRS FAKUR. Hysterical. Wants me to get on a plane to Paris.

SHIDEH. Did you tell him to stop his nagging?

MRS FAKUR. He booked me a ticket.

SHIDEH. Oh. When for?

MRS FAKUR. Tomorrow.

SHIDEH. Tomorrow.

MRS FAKUR. First thing.

SHIDEH *is speechless.* DORSA *walks in from the bedroom.*

DORSA. Maman, I need to go upstairs.

MRS FAKUR. What on earth is there upstairs?

DORSA. Kimia. They took her.

MRS FAKUR. I'm sure we'll find her once we've cleaned up this mess.

DORSA. Maman? I don't feel well.

SHIDEH *touches her forehead.*

SHIDEH. Oh you're burning up, Dor Dor.

DORSA. I want Kimia. They took her.

MRS FAKUR. Who took her?

DORSA. The djinn.

MRS FAKUR. Not you too, Dorsa.

SHIDEH. I promise we'll find her. Let's get you to bed.

DORSA *shakes her head and holds on to* SHIDEH.

Alright. Come here.

SHIDEH *carries* DORSA *to the sofa, tucks her in.* MRS FAKUR *takes* SHIDEH *to one side.*

MRS FAKUR. Shideh, maybe you should take that girl and get out of the city. Stay with your in-laws for a bit.

The doorbell rings. MRS FAKUR *picks up the bottle and glasses and takes them to the kitchen.* SHIDEH *answers it. It's* PARGOL

SHIDEH. Pargol. Come in.

PARGOL *enters.* MRS FAKUR *returns from the kitchen.*

MRS FAKUR. Oh Pargol, dear. How are you holding up?

PARGOL. I've just come to say goodbye.

SHIDEH. Come in and sit down.

MRS FAKUR. Where are you going?

PARGOL. Kurdistan.

MRS FAKUR. But it's so dangerous there.

PARGOL. It's where my dad wanted to be buried.

SHIDEH. You can stay here with us, Pargol, for as long as you need to.

PARGOL. Oh no, I don't want to stay in this horrible building one minute longer. There's something here, something awful.

DORSA *sits up on the sofa, she listens.*

MRS FAKUR. What on earth do you mean, my dear?

PARGOL *spots* DORSA *on the sofa.*

PARGOL. Dorsa? I need to speak to her.

SHIDEH. She's not feeling well.

PARGOL. Just for a minute. Please.

MRS FAKUR. She has a fever, Pargol.

PARGOL *sits next to* DORSA *on the sofa.*

PARGOL. Dorsa? Dorsa tell me what did you see yesterday?

DORSA *looks to her mum for help.*

SHIDEH. Pargol, please.

PARGOL. Dorsa remember the missile? You said you saw someone? I heard you.

DORSA *shakes her head.*

And you were crying, you were scared.

SHIDEH. Pargol joon.

PARGOL. What did you see Dorsa? Tell me. Aren't we friends?

DORSA *nods.*

Because my father, he saw something too, he was terrified, what did you see, Dorsa?

PARGOL *grabs hold of* DORSA*, shakes her.*

Dorsa, tell me please!

DORSA. Maman!

SHIDEH *tries to intervene. Pulls* PARGOL *off.*

SHIDEH. Pargol, please, you're upset, you're in shock.

PARGOL. I swear to you, right after that missile hit, he was totally fine, he was wide awake, sitting in his chair, alert, the missile was just sitting there right there in the middle of our living room, and he says to me, go and get me my walking stick, totally calm, totally normal, and I run to the other room to get his stick, but when I come back, he's as white as a sheet, and he's pointing, pointing at the corner of the room, totally transfixed, haunted, and whatever he was pointing at, that's what killed him. Wasn't it, Dorsa? Tell them. Tell them the truth.

MRS FAKUR. Your father died of a heart attack, Pargol.

PARGOL. There's something here. There's something here isn't there, Dorsa? Isn't there? Tell them. Tell them.

DORSA *nods.*

SHIDEH. That's enough, she's sick for God's sake.

PARGOL *turns to* SHIDEH

PARGOL. Why didn't you help me, Shideh?

MRS FAKUR. Let's go downstairs, dear.

PARGOL. You promised to help me, and then you sat there and said nothing. Why? Why?

SHIDEH. It wasn't my place, I'm sorry, Pargol, I'm –

PARGOL *starts to cry.* MRS FAKUR *gives her a hug.*

MRS FAKUR. It's okay, it's okay.

PARGOL. He would have listened to you. He would have listened to –

MRS FAKUR. Here, let's go downstairs. I'll make you some tea.

MRS FAKUR *escorts* PARGOL *out. They exit.*

SHIDEH. It's alright, Dor Dor. She's just very upset, okay? Do you want to watch one of your videos?

DORSA *nods.* SHIDEH *puts a video on. Cartoons. She closes the curtains, and joins* DORSA *on the sofa, cuddles her, strokes her hair.*

DORSA. Are we leaving?

SHIDEH. We'll see.

DORSA. We can't leave without Kimia because if we don't find her, I'll stay sick forever. Please, Maman.

SHIDEH. Just watch your cartoons, sweetheart. We'll find her. It's all going to be alright.

SHIDEH *and* DORSA *watch the TV together on the sofa. As they start to fall asleep, the video begins to warp. Darkness falls. The sounds of something scuttling across the Bijaris' apartment in the dark.*

SHIDEH *wakes up with a fright. It's dark, except for the glow from the static on the TV, and a small lamp.* DORSA *is fast asleep next to her.* SHIDEH *stands up and checks her watch, it's just before dawn. Suddenly the electricity goes out. The auditorium is plunged into total darkness.* SHIDEH *goes and gets some candles, lights a few and places them on a table. She walks back to the sofa but finds that* DORSA *is gone.* SHIDEH *panics, starts looking around for* DORSA. *The candles suddenly go out. Total darkness.*

There's a sudden, loud noise in the living room, like furniture moving or something falling over.

Dorsa?

We hear the noise again, closer this time.

Dorsa? Is that you?

SHIDEH *finds a torch. She turns it on. She very slowly scans the whole space, including the audience. She scans the living room, carefully scanning any nooks and crannies. Then the light catches something for just a second or two: A man. A creature. A djinn. He is naked. Maybe we glimpse his face for just a millisecond. Whatever we see, or think we've seen, it's horrifying.*

SHIDEH *drops the torch, and everything is plunged into total darkness again.*

ACT TWO

Scene One

Half an hour later. Dawn has broken. The apartment.

SHIDEH *wears a housecoat.* DORSA *is curled up on the sofa under a blanket. All the lights are on.* MR EBRAHIMI *stands in his pyjamas. He's annoyed and not doing very well at hiding it.*

MR EBRAHIMI. Nothing.

SHIDEH. I saw him. He was standing right there.

MR EBRAHIMI. Do you think maybe you could you have dreamt it?

SHIDEH. Can you check the big cupboard in the kitchen?

MR EBRAHIMI. Again?

> SHIDEH *nods.* MR EBRAHIMI *reluctantly exits to the kitchen. He returns.*

> It's strange it's only the women in this building who are hearing things.

SHIDEH. I didn't just hear something. I saw someone. With my own two eyes.

MR EBRAHIMI. My mother was always good at telling stories. Big imagination.

SHIDEH. There's still the bedrooms through there.

> MR EBRAHIMI *tries not to roll his eyes. He exits through the corridor. A few moments later, he returns.*

MR EBRAHIMI. All clear.

SHIDEH. Are you sure?

MR EBRAHIMI. There's no one here, no signs of a break-in, all the windows are locked.

SHIDEH. I was so sure I saw someone.

MR EBRAHIMI. You can stay in our spare room if you want?

SHIDEH. We'll be fine. Thank you, Mr Ebrahimi.

MR EBRAHIMI. And, Mrs Bozorgmehr, I'd appreciate you not telling my wife about this little nightmare you had.

SHIDEH. It wasn't a nightmare.

MR EBRAHIMI. She's been getting all worked up about djinn and silly old wives' tales, saying there's something in the building, and I can't afford to shut my shop up and leave, so don't spook her any further, if you don't mind.

SHIDEH. I won't say a word.

MR EBRAHIMI. Well. I'll be going then.

SHIDEH. Sorry for the trouble.

MR EBRAHIMI *heads to the door, then turns around.*

MR EBRAHIMI. Before I forget. Your car.

SHIDEH. What about it?

MR EBRAHIMI. Two of your wheels are flat. Didn't you notice? You better get someone round to sort it out.

MR EBRAHIMI *exits.*

SHIDEH *looks around, the morning light now fills the room. She checks* DORSA*'s temperature, she's fast asleep.*

A little bit of plaster from the cracks in the ceiling falls onto the floor. The doorbell rings.

SHIDEH *opens the door.* MRS FAKUR *stands in the doorway; she's wearing a headscarf and there is a suitcase at her feet. She holds out a Pyrex dish in her hands.*

MRS FAKUR. This one's definitely yours. I remember now, it was chipped.

SHIDEH *takes it.* MRS FAKUR *steps inside.*

SHIDEH. I was half hoping you'd change your mind.

MRS FAKUR. How's the fever?

SHIDEH. Still not broken.

MRS FAKUR. You haven't changed your mind? About your in-laws?

SHIDEH. A long journey is the last thing she needs right now.

MRS FAKUR. At least take her to a doctor, not that you're not, I mean, take her to a specialist, a pediatrician.

SHIDEH. Her doll's missing, I've looked everywhere, she says she won't get any better unless we find it, and I'm starting to think she might be telling the truth –

MRS FAKUR. Listen to me, Shideh. Take her to the doctor, get her some medicine, and she'll be better in no time, you'll see.

The sound of a taxi horn outside the building.

Well then. I guess it's goodbye.

SHIDEH. Do you think we'll see each other again?

MRS FAKUR. What a silly question. Of course we will.

SHIDEH. You promise you'll come back?

MRS FAKUR. First you go all superstitious and now you're being sentimental. Who are you and what have you done with my Shideh?

Taxi's waiting.

SHIDEH. Look after yourself.

MRS FAKUR. Oh don't fuss.

A pause.

I'll miss you.

SHIDEH *wells up.*

Will you be alright my dear?

SHIDEH *nods.*

Now stop crying, you're depressing me.

They hug goodbye. MRS FAKUR *leaves.* SHIDEH *locks the door.* DORSA *sits up.*

DORSA. Can I watch TV?

SHIDEH. Once I've done my exercises.

DORSA. But I'm sick.

SHIDEH. I won't be long my love.

DORSA *sulks and slumps onto the sofa.* SHIDEH *goes to the box of videos to get the Jane Fonda video tape. It's not there. She rummages around for it. No luck.*

Have you seen my workout tape?

DORSA. No.

SHIDEH *continues her search, maybe checks under the sofa, behind the bookshelf, but it's nowhere to be seen.*

SHIDEH. Where could it be?

DORSA. I'm not allowed to touch the tapes.

SHIDEH. I'm sure I put it back.

SHIDEH *looks in some drawers, tries the box of videos again. She gives up.*

Do want some breakfast?

DORSA *shakes her head.*

You need to eat or you won't get better, Dor Dor.

SHIDEH *exits into the kitchen.* DORSA *gets up and turns on the TV. She clicks the buttons, hops between the two channels, back and forth. She chooses a station and sits on the sofa.* SHIDEH *enters from the kitchen with a plate of toast, she stops to throw something in the bin – something catches her eye, she fishes out her Jane Fonda video, a messy nest of unspooled tape.* SHIDEH *storms over to* DORSA *brandishing the ruined video cassette.*

What is my workout tape doing in the bin?

DORSA *ignores her.*

Look at it. It's totally ruined.

DORSA *continues watching TV.*

I'm talking to you, Dorsa.

DORSA. Can we have chicken for lunch?

SHIDEH. Don't try and change the subject. I want to know why my tape is in the bin.

Answer me.

DORSA *stands up, walks over to the TV and turns the volume up.* SHIDEH *marches over to the TV and switches it off.*

DORSA. Hey!

SHIDEH. Go to your room.

DORSA *goes back to the sofa and crosses her arms.*

Now.

DORSA. I didn't do it!

SHIDEH. I am very upset Dorsa. Tell me the truth.

DORSA. They took Kimia, and they want something of yours too.

DORSA *stands up and walks back over to the TV, she reaches out to turn it on, her finger hovers over the button.*

SHIDEH. Don't you dare.

I'm warning you.

DORSA *hesitates, her finger hovers closer to the button, she glares at* SHIDEH.

Just try it.

DORSA *makes a run for the front door, she tries to open it, but finds it's locked. She starts banging her fists on it hard, urgently.* SHIDEH *rushes over.*

What are you doing? Stop it, Dorsa. Stop it NOW.

DORSA. I need to get Kimia.

DORSA *bangs even harder, starts kicking and screaming for Kimia.* SHIDEH *ties to restrain her, but* DORSA *pushes her off.* SHIDEH *grabs* DORSA *and drags her away from the door.*

SHIDEH. Why would she be up there? Stop it right now. STOP.

DORSA *makes another run for the door, but* SHIDEH *catches her.* DORSA *kicks* SHIDEH, *who raises her hand, as if to hit* DORSA. DORSA *cowers, then runs off towards the bedroom and exits.* SHIDEH *takes a deep breath, she grabs the ruined tape and throws it into the bin, then marches off towards the bedroom.*

Scene Two

The front door opens and a DOCTOR *walks in. He carries a doctor's bag and has a stethoscope round his neck.* SHIDEH *enters holding a very poorly* DORSA *by the hand.* SHIDEH *lifts her onto the dining table. The* DOCTOR *gets out an otoscope, and starts looking into* DORSA's *ears.*

DOCTOR. An Iranian, an American, and a German get on a plane. Lean a little to the left, sweetheart? But the plane crashes into the ocean and they all perish, and they're sent straight to hell. And now to the right? When they get there, the devil greets them and shows them to a payphone, he says, you each get one phone call home. And Ahhhhhh.

DORSA. Ahhhhhhhh –

DOCTOR. And again, but stick your tongue out.

DORSA. Ahhhhh –

DOCTOR. That's a good girl. So they each get up and take it in turns to call home.

The DOCTOR *picks up his stethoscope and starts examining* DORSA *'s back.*

When they're done, the devil charges the American one thousand dollars for his call – and breathe in, sweetheart – the German is charged two thousand dollars for his call, but the Iranian only has to pay one dollar for his. The American and German are outraged, and they start complaining to the devil, this is totally unfair, why was the Iranian charged so little?

He stops examining DORSA*, and turns to* SHIDEH*.*

And the devil leans in, grins a big evil grin and says, it's because he made a local call.

SHIDEH *chuckles.*

I forgot how hard you were to impress.

SHIDEH. I've heard about five different versions of that joke this year.

DOCTOR. Almost done now, sweetheart.

The DOCTOR *examines* DORSA *'s abdomen.*

DORSA. I lost my doll.

DOCTOR. Oh no, that's rubbish.

DORSA. If we don't find her, I'll get sicker and sicker.

SHIDEH. Dorsa.

DORSA. Then one night, Maman will put me to bed, and I'll never wake up.

SHIDEH. Sorry, she's just very sad about her doll. We'll find her, Dor Dor, don't worry.

The DOCTOR *tries to give* SHIDEH *a reassuring smile.*

DOCTOR. All done now, Dorsa joon.

He takes out a sweet and gives it to DORSA*. She takes it listlessly. He lifts her down from the table.* SHIDEH *strokes* DORSA *'s hair and sends her off, back to bed.* DORSA *exits to the bedroom.*

SHIDEH. I thought it might be her chest?

DOCTOR. Well there's no sign of internal infection.

SHIDEH. Then why isn't her fever breaking?

The DOCTOR *leans in.*

DOCTOR. Is everything okay, Shideh?

SHIDEH. Trying my best.

DOCTOR. Aren't we all. Everyone's under a lot of strain right now, and the kids, they absorb all that. I'm pretty sure her fever might be stress-related.

SHIDEH. It's hard not to worry. She's really not herself.

DOCTOR. Give it a few days. A change of scene might do her good?

What about you? How are you doing?

SHIDEH. I was fine until this fever.

DOCTOR. Must be a lot with Iraj away.

SHIDEH. Dorsa's counting the sleeps till he's back. Daddy's girl.

A beat.

DOCTOR. I was sorry to hear about your mother.

SHIDEH. Thank you. How are your kids? Two now?

DOCTOR. Three.

SHIDEH. Three? Wow.

The DOCTOR *takes out his wallet, opens it up and shows* SHIDEH *a picture.*

Oh, they're beautiful. Thanks for coming over at such short notice.

The DOCTOR *starts packing his instruments back into his bag.*

DOCTOR. You're lucky you caught me. I'm heading north first thing tomorrow. Roya and the kids are already there.

SHIDEH. We might do the same, once she's feeling better.

DOCTOR. Do you still hear from any of the others?

SHIDEH. Less and less.

DOCTOR. I've been meaning to ask, did you manage to get anywhere with the university?

SHIDEH *hesitates, unsure what to say. She shakes her head.*

I only mention it because, do you remember Abbas? They let him back in. He starts in a few weeks, with the new semester.

SHIDEH. Do you know how he did it?

DOCTOR. Apparently, he managed to get in front of the head of admissions. Pled his case. It worked.

SHIDEH. Thanks for taking a look at Dorsa.

DOCTOR. My pleasure. Anytime. Send my regards to Iraj.

The DOCTOR *picks up his bag and heads to the front door.*

And, Shideh. You were better than all of us. Don't give up alright?

The DOCTOR *exits.*

Scene Three

The radio bursts into life, the sound of the tannoy at the Student Selection Committee blares out, war propaganda music plays. SHIDEH *enters with headscarf, jacket and handbag. The* SECRETARY *walks in holding a clipboard.*

SHIDEH. I'm begging you, just let me speak to him, I only need a minute of his time, that's all I ask.

SECRETARY. I've already told you he's busy. His diary is full. You're wasting your time.

SHIDEH. My daughter is sick. My husband's serving in Ilam.

SECRETARY. God protect him. And if your daughter's sick, you should probably get back to her, shouldn't you?

SHIDEH. Finishing my studies is everything to me, it's all I have, please, let me see him, let me plead my case.

SECRETARY. Do you think yours is the first sob story I've heard?

SHIDEH. I'm just asking for a little bit of help, that's all.

SECRETARY. Help?

SHIDEH. Just a little help, sister.

SECRETARY. Listen, sister, for starters, I'd advise you to fix your headscarf, it's barely covering your hair. A woman should be more scared of exposing herself than anything else in the world. This is Tehran, not Paris. We have values now, and our men on the front are becoming martyrs to protect them. Their wives widowed. Their children orphaned. They're out there sacrificing their very lives with honour and dignity. And you think you can swan in here looking like that and ask for my help?

SHIDEH. I'm sorry.

SECRETARY. Perhaps if you'd have come in here showing a little more humility, a little more modesty, I'd have thought about helping you.

The SECRETARY *exits through the front door,* SHIDEH *watches her go, then hangs up her headscarf and handbag and jacket.*

Scene Four

SHIDEH *turns around and finds herself standing in front of* MRS EBRAHIMI. *The front door is open and* MRS EBRAHIMI *is standing in the hallway.*

MRS EBRAHIMI. She's been very restless. What did the doctor say?

SHIDEH. He said she's fine. No infection.

MRS EBRAHIMI. Why don't I brew some borage leaves for her?

SHIDEH. Don't trouble yourself, Mrs Ebrahimi, I've given her paracetamol.

MRS EBRAHIMI *lowers her voice.*

MRS EBRAHIMI. I'm not the kind of person who likes to spread rumours, but that thing didn't crash here by accident, you know. Of all the thousands of rooftops in Tehran, it falls on this one?

SHIDEH. There's a war on, / it's what happens –

MRS EBHRAHIMI. Oh it's no accident, trust me. It brought something with it.

SHIDEH. What?

MRS EBRAHIMI. I've been hearing strange noises at night. Haven't you? Whistling, scratching?

SHIDEH. Dorsa's been having nightmares. I'm sorry if she's / making noise –

MRS EBRAHIMI. Does she still talk about the…

MRS EBRAHIMI *leans in closer, almost whispers.*

Djinn?

SHIDEH *nods.*

They travel on the wind you know, just like that missile, and they only land once they find someone to possess.

SHIDEH. Why would they want to possess someone in this building?

MRS EBRAHIMI. They prey on the vulnerable. The elderly. The dying. On children.

SHIDEH. Are you suggesting they're here for Dorsa?

MRS EBRAHIMI. I heard Dorsa banging on the door yesterday, sounded like she was going to break it down. Like she was having some kind of fit.

SHIDEH. She's lost her doll, and she's convinced it's upstairs.

MRS EBRAHIMI. Oh God have mercy. If I was you, I would get a prayer locket and hang it round your daughter's neck this instant.

SHIDEH. Why would I need to do that?

MRS EBRAHIMI. When they take a personal belonging –

SHIDEH. Who?

MRS EBRAHIMI. The djinn. And if it's something you cherish, like Dorsa's doll, then that's it, there's no escape, they'll find you everywhere you go.

SHIDEH. And what if I can't find the doll? What if I never find it?

MRS EBRAHIMI. I don't want to scare you Mrs Bozorgmehr. But if you don't find it, then God protect you and your daughter.

SHIDEH. Why would they want to hurt her? Why Dorsa? It doesn't make any sense.

MRS EBRAHIMI. You educated lot think all your precious education, your logic and reason will save you. Trust me, not with this it won't.

SHIDEH. I just want her to get better.

MRS EBRAHIMI. You saw something didn't you?

SHIDEH *hesitates.*

You saw something with your own two eyes. I know it. Why else would you call Ebrahimi at dawn?

SHIDEH. I was half asleep / I –

MRS EBRAHIMI. There is a djinn in this building, Mrs Bozoghmer. It's as clear as day, all the signs are here

SHIDEH. What signs?

MRS EBRAHIMI. Didn't your mother teach you these things? Objects going missing? Unusual noises? Children acting strange, unexplained fevers, recurring nightmares, winds rising out of nowhere? Last night, I was tossing and turning all night long, couldn't fall asleep for the life of me, not a wink. Then suddenly, I hear a loud noise in the room. I sit up, wide awake. I listen. I wait. And, by God, I felt, with every bone in my body, that I was being watched.

MRS EBRAHIMI *takes hold of* SHIDEH*'s hand.*

Shideh, listen to me. They will hurt you and your daughter if you don't protect yourselves.

SHIDEH. How?

MRS EBHRAHIMI. They get into your head, play tricks on your mind. They can drive people to madness.

I wouldn't say all these things to you if I didn't know them to be true. For thousands of years they've been passed down, generation to generation, woman to woman. Because let me tell you this, in a crisis, it's women who watch. Even in this war, when the shells are raining down, It's the men who fall asleep first. They abandon themselves to fate. But us women, we stay up, we lie awake, and we worry, and we watch. And we see everything.

And I'm telling you, there is something in this building.

A moment of silence.

I brought you some esfand to burn. It will help. Here, take it.

MRS EBRAHIMI *hands* SHIDEH *a pack of esfand and a metal burner,* SHIDEH *takes it.*

SHIDEH. Thank you, Mrs Ebrahimi.

MRS EBRAHIMI. And Mrs Bozorgmehr, just between you and me, not that there's anyone's left in this damned building anyway, I've told Ebrahimi that it's better if we get the hell out of here. He needs a couple of days to get his shop in order. You should think about packing up and leaving too.

SHIDEH. But I can't leave without that doll.

MRS EBRAHIMI. I'll get you a prayer locket. Put it on Dorsa, that's the best we can do for now.

SHIDEH. Are you really leaving?

MRS EBRAHIMI. They say some of the martyrs are coming back with no heads, others with faces so disfigured it could only be the devil's work. I'm telling you those missiles are cursed, Mrs Bozorgmehr. I heard they're running out of men on the front, so they're having to send children. See what Saddam is doing to us? Children! Their eyes scorched, their little bodies bloated. I said to Ebrahimi, this baby is about to burst out of me, Mehdi is possessed, and Dorsa's next, and I can't sleep, and I can't eat, and you and your precious shop won't go bankrupt if you close up for a few weeks and leave the city.

SHIDEH. And what did he say?

MRS EBRAHIMI. He didn't say a word. He just walked off. But that's only because he knows I'm right.

MRS EBRAHIMI *exits.* SHIDEH *grabs the esfand burner, exits to the kitchen. Moments later she returns with the esfand alight. She stands under the hole in the ceiling, holding the burner under it. Smoke rises.*

Scene Five

Nighttime descends. SHIDEH *is still standing under the hole in the ceiling holding the esfand burner.*

Unseen by SHIDEH, *the front door is ajar. It's gently pushed open a little.* MEHDI *steps inside the doorway, silently.* MEHDI *watches* SHIDEH *as the smoke fills the room.* SHIDEH *turns around and sees him.*

SHIDEH. Mehdi. You gave me a fright. What are you doing here?

MEDHI *just stands there.*

Is everything alright?

MEHDI *doesn't respond, he takes a small step inside.*

Would you like to come in?

MEHDI *comes inside. He stares at* SHIDEH, *she puts the burner down.*

Do you want some water or juice?

MEHDI *shakes his head, no.*

Are you sure?

MEHDI *nods his head, yes.*

Dorsa's sleeping, Mehdi, she's got a fever.

MEDHI *stares at her for a few seconds, then looks at the esfand burner.* SHIDEH *follows his gaze.*

MEHDI. Are you scared?

SHIDEH *is taken aback.*

SHIDEH. No. It's just –

MEHDI *takes a few more steps in. Looks around the living room.*

Do you need something, Mehdi?

MEHDI. I want to say goodbye to Dorsa.

SHIDEH. Goodbye? Are you leaving?

MEHDI *shrugs.*

MEHDI. Dorsa said your mother's dead. Is it true?

SHIDEH. It is. She is.

MEHDI *spots a backgammon set on the cabinet. He goes over and opens it, fiddles with the pieces.*

I'm sorry about your mum. And your dad.

MEHDI. My mum used to play backgammon with me.

SHIDEH. Did she?

SHIDEH *picks up the backgammon set, puts it down on the coffee table for* MEHDI, *she closes the curtains, he kneels at the table.*

Did you win?

MEHDI *shakes his head.*

MEHDI. She was too good.

MEHDI *plays with the game pieces, lines them up, or makes a tower.*

SHIDEH. What else was she good at?

MEHDI *thinks.*

MEHDI. She was really good at jokes.

SHIDEH *smiles at him. He continues fiddling with the game.*

And when she peeled me an apple, the skin would all be in one piece, like a snake.

SHIDEH. That's impressive.

MEHDI. What could your mum do?

SHIDEH. My mum? Oh, I know, she was really good at making ice cream.

MEHDI. That's cool.

SHIDEH. In summer, she'd make a huge big bowl of it and hand it out to all our neighbours.

MEDHI. I can hold my breath underwater for almost two minutes.

SHIDEH. Oh wow.

MEHDI. I wanted to teach Dorsa but there's nowhere to swim.

MEHDI *stands up. He looks around.*

Can I go and play with Dorsa now?

SHIDEH. She's not very well Mehdi, she's resting.

MEHDI. Do you think I'm bad?

SHIDEH. No, of course not.

MEHDI. Because you know that time me and Dorsa were in your room. I was only showing her where to hide when the missile came.

SHIDEH. How did you know it was coming?

MEHDI. Did Dorsa find her doll?

SHIDEH. Do you know where it is? She's very sick, Mehdi.

MEHDI *shakes his head.*

MEHDI. If you don't find her doll, they'll come for her.

SHIDEH. Who told you all this?

MEHDI. You won't believe me.

SHIDEH. Mehdi, don't you want to help Dorsa? Isn't she your friend?

MEHDI. They came to my house first, and they told me.

SHIDEH. Have you seen them? Have you seen them in this building?

MEHDI *nods.*

Tell me where that doll is. I won't get you into any trouble. It will be our secret. I promise.

MEHDI. I should go now.

MEHDI *goes to leave.*

SHIDEH. Mehdi, please, help me. Where is that doll? We need it.

He turns around.

MEHDI. They want something of yours. They took Dorsa's doll and they'll take something of yours if you aren't careful.

SHIDEH. Something like what?

MEHDI. Your book. The one your mother gave you.

SHIDEH. Did Dorsa tell you about the book?

MEHDI *shakes his head. Then looks up at the crack in the ceiling, to the Bijaris'. He walks to the door and opens it, before he steps out he turns to* SHIDEH.

MEHDI. My mum told me I shouldn't ever lie. So I would never.

MEHDI *leaves.* SHIDEH *shuts the door behind him. She runs over to the chest of drawers in the living room, fishes out the key from its hiding place and opens her special drawer. The book is there. She looks at it, touches the words her mother wrote her. The phone rings.* SHIDEH *jumps. She puts the book back, closes the drawer, and locks it. She rushes over to the phone and picks it up. The audience can make out most of what* IRAJ *is saying on the other side of the line.*

SHIDEH. Hello?

IRAJ. *Shideh?*

SHIDEH. Oh, Iraj! Oh, thank God. I've been losing my mind, I've been so worried. Are you okay?

IRAJ. *I'm fine, the lines have been down. Are you and Dorsa okay? What's this about a missile?*

SHIDEH. It's so good to hear your voice, Iraj. We miss you. I miss you.

IRAJ. *What the hell are you still doing there? Will you stop being so selfish for once in your life –*

SHIDEH. I want to leave, but we can't –

The TV comes on, IRAJ *appears on it, his face, close-up.* SHIDEH *stares.* IRAJ*'s voice no longer comes out of the phone, but from the television, his image flickers and distorts, his voice is crackly, comes in snatches, but we can still make out most of what he says.* SHIDEH *rushes over to the TV, she speaks to it, touches the screen.*

IRAJ. *Stop being so fucking stubborn and go to my parents. Now.*

SHIDEH. Dorsa has a fever and it won't break. It's been days.

IRAJ. *Just go north, Shideh. I beg you.*

SHIDEH. I've tried everything, but nothing's working.

IRAJ. *I'll come and get her myself.*

SHIDEH. I don't want to move her when she's burning up like this, and she needs her doll.

IRAJ. *What doll?*

SHIDEH. We can't find Kimia. And we can't leave without her, Iraj. They want to hurt her.

IRAJ. *What the hell are you talking about?*

SHIDEH. You haven't been here. You wouldn't understand. If we don't find it, she'll get worse and worse. She might never wake up.

IRAJ. *Listen to me you stupid bitch.*

SHIDEH. Iraj?

IRAJ. *I'll take her away from you and you'll never see her again. You don't even want her, you never wanted her, you don't fucking deserve her.*

SHIDEH. Stop.

IRAJ. *You don't deserve this family, you're a selfish piece of shit, do you hear me?*

SHIDEH. Please don't.

IRAJ. *I'll take her far away and you'll never see her again. Because deep down that's what you really want? Isn't it? To be rid of her? Free of her? Isn't it?*

SHIDEH. Iraj, please.

The image and sound on the screen starts flickering on and off and cutting out, IRAJ *disappears from the screen, and the TV turns off. Suddenly – a tapping on the window.* SHIDEH *listens carefully. Another tap tap at the window.*

SHIDEH freezes. Another tap. SHIDEH walks over towards the window and the tapping stops. She builds up the courage to open the curtains – and there's nothing there. She catches her breath.

DORSA. MAMAN! MAMAN! I've been sick.

SHIDEH goes off to the bedroom.

The lights flicker on and off.

Suddenly, in the hallway, a terrifying figure in a long black chador appears out of nowhere for just a moment and then vanishes.

The lights cut out.

Scene Six

The lights come back on, SHIDEH *and* DORSA *sit on the sofa,* MRS EBRAHIMI *looms over them.*

MRS EBRAHIMI. Has her fever broken?

SHIDEH. Her fever?

MRS EBRAHIMI. Are you feeling alright, Mrs Bozghomer?

SHIDEH. It's still there. She hasn't eaten in days.

MRS EBRAHIMI. Here, I brought you a prayer locket. Take it.

MRS EBRAHIM hands SHIDEH *the prayer locket.* SHIDEH *takes it.* DORSA *sits up on the sofa and listens.*

SHIDEH. Will this be enough?

MRS EBRAHIMI. Listen, we're heading north tonight. Why don't you come with us?

SHIDEH. That's so kind of you, thank you. I don't want to impose?

MRS EBRAHIMI. Impose? I see you more than I see my own family. We can drop you off at your in-laws.

SHIDEH. I want to go with you, but I can't leave without that doll, Mrs Ebrahimi.

DORSA *gets up from the sofa, she's lethargic and groggy. She walks over and hugs* SHIDEH*'s legs, and holds on to her hand.*

MRS EBRAHIMI. I really don't want to leave you here all on your own, and with no car. Hello, sweetie. And don't you worry if I find out Mehdi had anything to do with those tyres, I'll ring his neck until it snaps.

SHIDEH. We can get a bus –

MRS EBRAHIMI. Are you crazy, the queues are unbelievable, there's an exodus. And those bus drivers drive like madmen. I wouldn't get on one if you paid me. Why don't you just come with us?

SHIDEH. Okay. Okay. Thank you, Mrs Ebrahimi, thank you so much.

DORSA. No, Maman, we can't go. We can't.

MRS EBRAHIMI. Don't you worry, Dorsa. I got you this special necklace.

MRS EBRAHIMI *takes the prayer locket from* SHIDEH, *bends down and puts in on* DORSA.

There we are. You're going to be alright, sweetie.

DORSA. Maman, please.

MRS EBRAHIMI. I better get back to packing. And, Mrs Bozorgmehr, Mr Ebrahimi says this might be a long one, so get your affairs in order, who knows when we'll be back.

MRS EBRAHIMI *moves towards the door.* SHIDEH *grabs Dorsa's jacket and shoes from the coat rack, puts it on her.*

DORSA. Where are we going?

SHIDEH. I have to do something important before we leave, my love.

MRS EBRAHIMI. Make sure you're back before five, because Mr Ebrahimi won't wait for anyone, and I'm telling you he's the most stubborn man in Tehran.

MRS EBRAHIMI *exits.*

SHIDEH *puts* DORSA*'s shoes on. She's too weak to resist.*

DORSA. Everything hurts.

SHIDEH. We won't be long.

SHIDEH *takes the black chador from the coat rack and puts it on. She grabs her handbag and* DORSA*'s hand and runs out the door.*

Scene Seven

The office of the Director of the Student Selection Committee, framed picture of Ayatollah Khomeini, Iran's Supreme Leader, take centre-stage. The DIRECTOR *enters, holding a file, papers.* SHIDEH *rushes in behind him, dragging an exhausted* DORSA*. The* SECRETARY *bursts behind* SHIDEH*. The* DIRECTOR *doesn't look up from his work.*

SHIDEH. Hello, sir.

SECRETARY. Where do you think you're going?!

SHIDEH. Sir, I just need a minute of your time, I've been waiting for hours

SECRETARY. OUT! Right now!

SHIDEH. And all I'm asking is that you reconsider –

DORSA *tugs at her mother's arm.* SHIDEH *scoops her up and carries her.*

SECRETARY. I'm so sorry sir, she just stormed in, I couldn't stop her.

SHIDEH. My name is Shideh Bozor–

DIRECTOR. I know exactly who you are.

The DIRECTOR *still doesn't look up.*

Take the child outside.

And close the door.

The SECRETARY *obeys, she walks over to* SHIDEH, *who hands* DORSA *over.* DORSA *resists and grabs hold of her mother, fearfully.* SHIDEH *whispers some reassurances and reluctantly hands her over,* DORSA *struggles and reaches out for her mum as the* SECRETARY *carries her away.* SHIDEH *turns to the* DIRECTOR, *tongue-tied.*

Well then? Speak.

SHIDEH. Sir, you see, I just want to return to my studies. There's nothing more important to me in the whole world. It's what I'm meant to do, it's my calling, I'm meant to be a doctor, sir, serving society, serving my community, it's always been my only ambition in life and I'd be lost without it, I'm already lost without it. How can my future be destroyed like this, just because of one mistake?

DIRECTOR. So, you admit it?

SHIDEH. Admit what, sir?

DIRECTOR. Your mistake.

SHIDEH. Don't we all make mistakes? Aren't we all just human, sir?

DIRECTOR. And what was your mistake?

SHIDEH. If only I knew the details of my case I would tell you.

DIRECTOR. Surely you know what it is that you have done, because it is you who did it.

SHIDEH. I'm assuming this is all because I was politically active.

DIRECTOR. That's one way of putting it.

SHIDEH. But sir, wasn't everyone involved in politics during the revolution? I was just young and naive…

The DIRECTOR *looks out of the window.*

I was clueless, I didn't even understand the difference between left and right back then, I just got swept up in it all, like everyone else. I love my country and I wanted change, I wanted progress, surely you understand?

The DIRECTOR *doesn't react. He is stone cold.*

And if I ended up in one of those radical leftist groups, it was only because I didn't know any better, I was immature, gullible, but I've changed now. I'm a wife, a mother, I have a daughter. I see things differently now, and I regret it all with all my heart.

DIRECTOR. Every mistake has its consequences. Every action, its reaction.

SHIDEH. Nothing means more to me in the world than my studies, than becoming a doctor. Nothing.

DIRECTOR. Not even your daughter?

SHIDEH. Please don't take this away from me. I beg you. Forgive me. Forgive me, please. I'll do whatever it takes.

DIRECTOR. I only let you in so that you can hear it directly from the horse's mouth, and so you stop wasting your time hounding us with your ridiculous letters and all your desperate pleading. Listen to me carefully. Read my lips. You will never continue your studies. And based on your sordid history there is not even the slightest chance in hell that you can ever return to the university. So, I suggest you pick yourself up, go home to your family, and find a new goal in life. Because your medical career, Mrs Bozorgmehr, is utterly, completely, and irrevocably, over. It is dead in the water. Forever. Now get out.

The DIRECTOR *stands up and walks towards* SHIDEH, *she backs away slowly, keeping her eyes trained on him. The* DIRECTOR *gets closer.* SHIDEH *turns and runs. The* DIRECTOR *follows after her. They exit.*

Scene Eight

SHIDEH *bursts through the front door, wearing her chador, her coat and handbag. She pulls* DORSA *by her arm. She sits* DORSA *down on the sofa.*

SHIDEH. Wait here.

DORSA. Don't leave me.

SHIDEH. I'll be right back, sweetheart.

SHIDEH *exits. She goes down the stairwell. She calls out for* MRS EBRAHIMI. DORSA *hugs herself on the sofa, fearfully. We hear* SHIDEH*'s voice echoing in the empty building. A few moments later,* SHIDEH *returns.*

Shit.

SHIDEH *rushes off to the bedroom and returns with a duffel bag, she opens a drawer, throws in some items.*

DORSA. What about Kimia?

SHIDEH *kneels down and holds* DORSA*'s face.*

SHIDEH. Listen to me. Where did you last see her?

DORSA *points at the dining table.* SHIDEH *goes and looks around the table, moves the chairs*

Where else could she be?

DORSA *points at the sofa,* SHIDEH *looks under the sofa, throws cushions onto the floor. Nothing,*

Don't worry my love. We'll find her together, and as soon as we find her, we'll get out of here. Is that a deal?

DORSA *nods.* SHIDEH *starts to look around the living room, she checks under the sofa, behind the cushions.* DORSA *joins in, looks through her toybox. As the search goes on,* SHIDEH *grows more frustrated, the search becomes more frantic, she starts turning the place upside down.*

Go and look in your room.

DORSA *exits to her bedroom.* SHIDEH *continues her search, she pulls out drawers and empties their contents onto the floor, she moves furniture to look under it. She pulls out the toybox and turns it upside down, its contents tumble out across the floor, the place begins to look ransacked.*

DORSA *returns empty handed. Something has shifted in her.*

I can't find her. I don't know what to do any more, Dorsa. I don't know what to do!

DORSA. Look harder!

SHIDEH. It's no good, Dorsa. She isn't here. We have to go now.

DORSA. No!

SHIDEH. We'll find her when we come back, I promise.

DORSA *returns to searching, she opens the cabinet, throws things on the floor and at* SHIDEH.

We have to stop now. We can't look forever. We're leaving. Stop. Stop. Enough.

DORSA *stares intently at the ceiling. A little bit of plaster and dust falls down from the crack in the ceiling.* SHIDEH *notices and looks up, scratching noises can be heard, then the sound of something scuttling across the floor upstairs, the lights in the apartment flicker.*

A knock on the door.

SHIDEH *gestures to* DORSA *to stay quiet. They wait and listen in silence for a few beats.* DORSA *follows something moving across the room.*

DORSA. There's a lady.

SHIDEH. What lady?

DORSA. She's right there.

SHIDEH. There's no one here.

One of Shideh's course books suddenly falls out of its place on the shelves behind her. Then another. SHIDEH spins around and grabs a pair of scissors from a drawer for protection.

DORSA. She comes and speaks to me when you're not around.

SHIDEH. There's no one here Dorsa.

Another object falls off a shelf on the other side of the room.

DORSA. She says you know where Kimia is.

SHIDEH. She isn't real, Dorsa, this is all in your head.

DORSA. She's standing right there.

SHIDEH. Look at me.

DORSA. She says you hid Kimia from me on purpose.

SHIDEH. I didn't take her. I promise.

DORSA. She says she saw you slashing the tyres in the garage.

SHIDEH. Dorsa don't listen to her. She's lying. Don't look at her.

DORSA. You're a horrible mother.

SHIDEH. What did you say?

DORSA. You heard me.

SHIDEH. Stop it.

DORSA. You're not a real doctor, you're a terrible mother, you're just a failure.

SHIDEH. Be quiet.

DORSA. Baba hates you.

SHIDEH *grabs* DORSA *roughly by the shoulders.*

SHIDEH. He doesn't

DORSA. Your mother hated you.

SHIDEH. Don't say that.

DORSA. And I hate you. With all my heart.

SHIDEH *slaps* DORSA *across the face.* DORSA *is stunned into silence.* SHIDEH *instantly regrets what she's done.* DORSA *rubs her cheek.*

SHIDEH. I'm sorry, my darling, I'm so sorry.

SHIDEH *goes to hug* DORSA*, but she cowers in fear.* DORSA *backs away towards the front door.*

I'm sorry. I didn't mean to. Dorsa!

DORSA *opens the door and runs out, her footsteps can be heard going up the stairwell.* SHIDEH *gets up and starts running towards the door after* DORSA.

Come back!

Just as SHIDEH *reaches the door, it slams shut in her face. She tries to open it, but it's locked. We hear* DORSA*'s voice offstage screaming for help.*

DORSA (*offstage*). *MAMAN! HELP ME PLEASE!*

SHIDEH. DORSA! I'm coming. Open the door!

SHIDEH *bangs on the door,* DORSA *continues to scream.* SHIDEH *tries with all her strength to get the door to open.*

DORSA *enters from the bedroom.*

DORSA. Maman? What's going on?

SHIDEH *spins around. She holds up the scissors.*

SHIDEH. Stay away from me.

DORSA. Maman, you're scaring me.

SHIDEH. You aren't real.

DORSA*'s screams are heard from the stairwell.*

DORSA! I'm coming! I'm coming!

DORSA. I'm Dorsa, Maman, I'm Dorsa.

SHIDEH. You aren't my daughter.

SHIDEH *brandishes the scissors again.*

DORSA. Don't say that, please, it's me.

SHIDEH. You're one of them.

DORSA. It's me, it's me, Maman, it's Dor Dor.

DORSA comes towards her mother.

SHIDEH. Get away from me!

SHIDEH pulls at the handle. The door finally gives, SHIDEH falls out into the hallway, she gets up and runs up the stairs. DORSA's screaming stops.

Dorsa where are you? DORSA?

DORSA. Maman come back!

DORSA is now all alone in the flat, a wind begins to blow, papers fly, the curtains billow. DORSA cowers in a corner. Suddenly a figure in a giant billowing black chador appears out of nowhere in the middle of the living room, for a split second we get a glimpse of her, she has a huge pregnant belly, swollen, almost bursting.

The figure vanishes, and DORSA runs away towards door to escape. But the figure appears again, climbing out of the TV.

DORSA runs back towards the bedroom, but out of nowhere the figure in the chador appears in the hallway, we glimpse it for a second, before it retreats into the darkness.

DORSA, terrified, takes a few steps backwards. SHIDEH bangs on the door. Out of the darkness, the figure holds out Kimia. We can just about make out the arm, and fingers, a little too long to be human, holding the doll, half-hidden in the shadows. DORSA stares, then takes a few steps towards Kimia.

The door gives way and SHIDEH tumbles into the apartment. She spots DORSA, who has stepped into the shadows, reaching for the doll. SHIDEH tries to step towards her, but the wind is too strong.

SHIDEH. DORSA, NO! Come here. Don't go to her.

DORSA. You ran away from me.

SHIDEH. I was confused.

DORSA. You never wanted me.

SHIDEH. That's not true. I want you, I've always wanted you. Listen to me, Dorsa.

DORSA. She says she wants me. She loves me. She wants to play.

DORSA *goes closer to the figure in the darkness, she reaches out for the doll.*

SHIDEH. NO! DORSA! Listen to me, listen –

DORSA. She says you're always sad. Because I make you sad.

SHIDEH. I'm not sad.

DORSA. Yes you are, and it's because of me.

SHIDEH. No, Dor Dor, it's not because of you. I'm sad because, it's because –

DORSA. You never tell me anything.

DORSA *takes the doll.*

The lady tells me everything. She loves me.

SHIDEH. NO! Please Dorsa come back to me, please, I'm trying to be happy, I try so hard to be happy, and I wish you were enough, but I'm so lonely, I'm all alone, Dorsa, Maman is all alone and I hate it, I hate it, I hate it. I need more than this, I need more, it's not enough, this isn't enough

DORSA *step towards the figure in the shadows.*

They took everything from me, everything, all of it, my studies, my work, my life, everything I knew is gone, they stripped me bare, can't you see that I have nothing? I am nothing. Can't you see that there's nothing left of me, Dorsa? Everything is lost. Everything. They won. They won. They won.

The figure reaches out a hand, it's long, too long for a human being. DORSA *takes it.*

Even my mother is gone. Oh Maman, I miss her, I miss my mother, Dorsa. Where is she? Where did she go? Sometimes I look for her, but she's not here. She's not here any more. I want her. I miss her. I just want my mother, Dor Dor.

DORSA *lets go of the hand.*

But none of it matters. None of it matters. Because I love you. I love you. I love you.

DORSA *runs to* SHIDEH *and straight into her arms.*

SHIDEH *catches her. The woman vanishes.*

The wind settles. Everything subsides.

SHIDEH *and* DORSA *remain in an embrace.*

SHIDEH *strokes* DORSA*'s hair, kisses her head, she smells her hair, she rocks her.* DORSA *clutches Kimia.*

I love you.

I love you, Dorsa.

So much.

I love you.

I love you.

I'm so sorry.

Oh, Dorsa.

My Dor Dor.

I love you.

Let's go.

Let's go far away.

Me and you.

Far far away.

SHIDEH *holds* DORSA *until the dawn light breaks through the window.*

Your fever. It's gone. Oh, my love.

DORSA. Can we go now?

SHIDEH gets up, grabs the duffel bag, zips it up.

Don't forget Grandma's special book.

SHIDEH goes to her drawer. She opens it. The book is gone. She takes the drawer out, holds it upside down. Nothing.

SHIDEH. It's gone.

SHIDEH grabs DORSA's hand, puts her's and DORSA's coats on, picks up the bag. They are about to leave, when the transistor radio bursts into life, as the red alert siren wails. DORSA looks at SHIDEH in terror.

Everything will be alright. Don't worry.

DORSA curls up in SHIDEH's lap.

As soon as the siren stops, we'll leave. We'll go to Grandma's. It will be over soon.

SHIDEH strokes DORSA's hair.

DORSA. Can I have a story?

As SHIDEH speaks, the light gradually starts to fade, until we only see her head and shoulders, then just her face, then just her eyes and mouth.

SHIDEH. When the shelling stops. We'll run down the stairs and straight to the mechanic, and he'll come round and change the wheels, all shiny and new. Then we climb into the car. At first the ignition doesn't start and we panic. I try again and again and then to our delight the car bursts into life. And we both cheer. We drive out of the garage. And into the light.

We drive through the early morning streets of Tehran. And as we drive north on the open road, the dawn sky blooms. It's orange and purple and red all at once. The horizon is empty, it's all just for us. We are mesmerised.

We see missiles in the distance and we watch as they turn into glittering fireworks.

You make up jokes to tell your grandma, and we laugh and you get the giggles. You ask me to tell you about the day you were born, and I tell you that all I can remember is that it was the first day of rain after summer, and your face, your tiny little face.

We turn on the radio. Pop music. It's your favourite song. I turn it up full volume. We open the windows. And the wind blows in our hair.

And when we get to the turning on the road that leads to your grandparents' house, I look over, and you've fallen asleep, Dorsa, and I look out at the horizon, and it calls to me, it calls to both of us, and I keep going and I keep going and I keep going. And I drive. And I drive. I drive. Drive away. Drive away. And away. And over. Over. Over and across. Across the border. And away. And away.

Away. Away. Away.

Away. Away.

Away.

The darkness engulfs them.

End.